D0944053

What Time's the Next Swan?

What Time's the Next Swan?

by Walter Slezak

(as told to Smith-Corona Model 88E)

Doubleday & Company, Inc.
Garden City, New York, 1962

Library of Congress Catalog Card Number 62–17357

Printed in the United States of America

To the sunlight that brightens the
autumn of my life—

To my wife

Don't blame me! Blame Jean Kerr. Just because, through the years, she heard me make caustic and irreverent remarks, remarks that SHE thought funny, that dear heart chose to believe that I am a wit and raconteur.

This book is her idea. She got me into it. She got Doubleday into it, and if you, dear readers, as I fervently hope you will, buy this book—she got you into it also.

On May 26, from here on referred to as the "day of conception" Doubleday invited me to lunch and told me of Jean's rash and irresponsible belief that "there was a book in me."

They offered me a contract with a large advance. All my life I've been unable to resist cash, so—money-mad idiot that I am—I nodded and the course of my placid life was changed.

Since the "day of conception" I haven't read a book, I haven't played a game of chess, I haven't enjoyed entertainment or a moment's relaxation without having a king-sized guilt complex about not "writing."

All kinds of methods were suggested.

"Tell whatever you have to say to some talented writer; it will then become a professional job, with just a small footnote that reads "AS TOLD TO —"

But my pride as a do-it-yourself man rebelled against that. I also discovered, that "AS TOLD TO —" would share in the royalties. That thought I found highly unattractive.

"Hire a ghost writer. He won't get credit, you pay him a flat fee, and at least the book will come out in fairly good English." I didn't like the vagueness of "flat fee," and who wants to read a book in fairly good English anyway, so I dropped that idea fast.

"You are an actor—you need an audience; invite a few friends to your house, tell them the story of your life and have a tape recorder going while you do it." That was a glorious idea. My friends co-operated magnificently. Their loyal laughter greeted every word I uttered. It made me terribly self-conscious, and after two sessions I ran out of friends.

Next I got myself a transistor-powered little sound-scriber, small enough to fit into one's pocket. The sales pitch was impressive: "If you are in a car, in a plane, on the beach—yes, even in the privacy of your bathtub and you *should* get an idea (the salesman stressed the word "should")—just press a little button, hold the mike close to your mouth and—away you go. It will all be there on a small plastic disc. When you've had your say, you slip the disc into an air-mail envelope and mail it to your secretary." It sounded great, except that I have no secretary, and, holding that monstrous little mike close to my mouth, I never did get an idea.

My thirteen-year-old son Leo came up with an ingenious solution: he suggested paper and pencils. I soon learned that the ratio of writing to chewing is about one to eight. Not to my dying day shall I forget the taste of Eberhard Faber, Mongol No. 2—with that savory rubber eraser flavor at the end. Just before this book went to press, I figured out that I have eaten about a hundred eighty-three yards of pencils, all without ill effect.

"Overwrite—put down everything that comes to your mind," I was told.

"Be explicit, elaborate. Judicious pruning will be done later. Don't be afraid to name names. Lawyers will tooth-comb the book before it gets into print and protect you from libel suits. Don't be afraid to shock people. Be daring. Be spicy. Tell all!"

I did.

I followed everybody's advice. About seven hundred thirty pages were judiciously pruned in order to protect the innocent, to make it possible for the book to be sent through the U.S. mails, and to prevent me from spending the twilight years of my life in jail for criminal libel.

What's left is here.

PLEASE LIKE IT.

What Time's the Next Swan?

1. BIOGRAPHIES USUALLY BEGIN with the smack on the bottom and the first lusty cry of the subject. I deplore this literary custom, because it is impossible to remember anything about one's birth firsthand. It is bound to be hearsay, and embellished, gilded hearsay at that.

I have been told that I made my initial appearance in this wonderful world on May 3, 1902, at 1:41 A.M.; the country was Austria, the city Vienna, the address Elisabethstrasse No. 5. and the exact location the bedroom of my parents on the fourth floor, overlooking the famous Confisserie Uhl.

The proximity of that emporium of calorie-laden delicacies may have been a contributing factor to my latter-day obesity.

The event was witnessed and attended by a doctor, a midwife, and assorted female relatives, and presided over by my maternal grandmother, who, having given birth to five children of her own, considered herself an expert, loaded with know-how.

I was born into an atmosphere of strife and tension. Grandmother constantly criticized the ministrations of the midwife, who threatened to quit. She belittled the professional opinion of the obstetrician, who ordered her out of the room.

Papa had also been ordered out of the room for being an all-around nuisance.

At last I let out my first yell, was bathed, and was presented to him. He was wild with joy.

"It's got a tassel!" he shouted. "I have a baby with a

tassel!" And he held me up to the electric light to get the first admiring look at me.

With the atavistic instinct of an old tigress defending her litter, my grandmother snatched me from his hands and accused him of trying to blind me.

He, with the atavistic instinct and inbred animosity of generations of sons-in-law, snatched me right back and declared that a little light certainly wouldn't hurt *his* child.

She grabbed me and called him criminally insane.

He grabbed me right back and called her an old dragon. With every ensuing epithet I was passed back and forth like a football, until the midwife rescued me.

The night before I was born my father had sung the part of Walther von Stolzing in Richard Wagner's opera *Die Meistersinger von Nuernberg.* So the name of "Walter" was chosen for me.

I have never been able to find out why the H was omitted from my given name, but I am grateful that it was, because with the American passion for abbreviations I would today not be called "Walt," which is bad enough, but "Walth," which sounds like an imperative sentence or at best a lisp.

During the first year of my life liquid nourishment was dispensed to me through the courtesy of a wet nurse. She was a simple Hungarian peasant girl named Ilona Gabor (no relation).

I was often told that her milk-producing attachments were of fabulous and joyous proportions.

Habits acquired in childhood are hard to break, and happy traumas followed me for the rest of my life.

Dr. Genser, our pediatrician, concerned that Ilona's milk should be nourishing and free of irritants, had prescribed a strict diet for her. But dear, full-blown Ilona cheated.

Secretly she ate hot peppers, spiced salami, bacon with paprika and doused all her food with the Hungarian equivalent of tabasco sauce.

The results soon appeared. They appeared on my face and my body. I broke out in crimson rashes and looked like a baby Lazarus. Whenever I was taken to the park in my perambulator, I was attired like Salome: seven veils, to hide my repulsiveness.

Salves, ointments, and powders were lavished on my eczema-ridden little body. All to no avail.

In 1902 the science of allergies was not as progressed as it is today, where it supports a vast amount of specialists in exorbitant luxury. Scratch tests, at five bucks a scratch, were unknown and the good Dr. Sigmund Freud had not then given psychosomatic sicknesses as excuses to doctors who couldn't find a cure.

It was my grandmother's eagle eye and fine sleuthing that finally unmasked Ilona as the carrier of my affliction. Horrible scenes of vengeance and retribution took place, the poor girl became a ward of Grandmother, and all her culinary trespasses were stopped.

After one week the rashes disappeared, my pink and rosy complexion was restored, I was unveiled and was again displayed, full of pride, for everyone to admire my beauty.

In that wonderful musical show *Knickerbocker Holiday* Maxwell Anderson defined the outstanding characteristics of an American as "one who refuses to take orders!"

I think that I qualified for that, my chosen nationality, at an early age. As far back as I can remember, an expressly given order triggered instant defiance. My little mind started functioning like an IBM machine; signals flashed in my resistance center, lights flickered around my resentment glands, bell and buzzer alerted all the cunning of a five-year-old.

Strategy and tactics went to work, not to rest till they had circumvented or defied that specific order.

I don't know if that character trait was deplorable or laudable; I only know that I have never been able to lose it. And I am extremely grateful that I was too young to serve in the First World War and too old for the Second; I surely would have been court-martialed for insubordination, and expired in front of a firing squad.

Even today, at my ripe old age, if someone suggests I do something and this suggestion is tinged with an excessive amount of authority, I immediately turn into a bristling fortress of resistance.

Needless to say that I have spent a large part of my childhood behind the eight ball.

The first act of flagrant disobedience I can recall happened during one of our summer vacations in a small village in the Austrian Tyrol called Brixlegg. My parents had rented several rooms in an old farmhouse.

Farmhouses in most of Europe are very compact and built with great efficiency. Only the front part of the house is used for human habitation. The larger hind part contains the stables on the ground floor, over them the barn, where hay and feed are kept. Behind the house is the dung heap.

The higher the dung heap is filled, the more prosperous the farmer is considered to be.

The rooms were very small and had extremely low ceilings, a fact my poor father was reminded of several times a day. Every time he straightened his six foot seven frame or walked through a door, he crashed head-first into some beam. He cursed, wailed, moaned in pain, and loudly deplored the fact that, instead of a house, he had rented an undersized monkey cage.

This prompted the farmer's wife, our landlady, to remark acidly that her home was not meant to house giraffes.

I was five years old and had long blond curls. They were daily brushed and combed and I hated them. All the other kids made fun of me; I cried and had tantrums, until the final order was given: no haircut until I was six years old and ready for school.

That afternoon, while everybody was having his siesta, I sneaked out of the house and ran down to the village into the barbershop. I announced that Papa wanted me to have a haircut and that he would come by later and pay for the job.

I must have been a convincing liar, because the rustic Figaro set me into a high stool and the ravishment of my virginal hirsuteness began. My head felt cool and comfortable.

I ran home, thrilled with my courage and trembling with fear. My reception justified my fear.

Mama cried that her child had been despoiled: she dragged me to a mirror and forced me to see what I had done to HER: my head looked like a billiard ball with a three days' growth of stubble beard. The ears protruded like handles on a jug, and my eyes, mouth, and nose, which had formerly been so delicately framed by my curls, looked coarse and foreign.

Papa didn't cry; but he gave me the first serious spanking of my life. For the next two days I was not allowed to eat at the table with the rest of the family, no desserts—and whenever they caught sight of me, murderous disapproving looks were shot my way.

But then something happened that made my escapade seem small and unimportant.

All during the previous weeks it had been raining steadily, day in and day out—strings of water pouring down like a curtain of transparent spaghetti; the river below our house had begun to rise dangerously. There was a lot of worried talk about impending disaster and the first evidence of a catastrophe somewhere upstream floated past our house: uprooted trees, a few pieces of furniture, the roof of a barn, a drowned cow, and a dog.

The dog was a small, yellow-colored mutt, furiously swimming and yelping, and I couldn't understand why no one jumped into the swirling waters to rescue him.

I remember that my parents packed all our bags, ready to evacuate us to higher grounds. In the evening we were put to bed with our clothes on, but didn't fall asleep for a long time: the roar of the water, the voices, the flickering of lanterns and torches—it was all very frightening.

The next morning at daybreak we all huddled together on the balcony. The river had risen seven feet during the night and was licking at our front door. The lower part of the house was awash and the stables flooded. Huge waves, dirty muddy yellow brown rolled by—when suddenly I heard Papa declare dramatically that if the waters subsided he would give a charity concert for the benefit of the stricken population.

The good Lord must have heard his stentorian voice and considered it a good bargain, because it suddenly stopped raining, the sun came up, and by evening the river had started to recede.

I was terribly impressed with the pull Papa had in the very top echelon and have since then made many vows myself—though not always with such spectacular results.

The concert was given in the nearby town of Innsbruck and must have been a huge financial success, because Papa was treated like a hero and was made an honorary citizen of Brixlegg.

Our landlady, puffed up with pride that such a benefactor and great celebrity should be living under her roof, promptly raised our rent.

The next time I asserted my independence was during the great and solemn ceremony of the official opening of

Vienna's new concert hall, the Grosser Concert Haus Saal.

The ritual started with a benediction, and then the last movement of Beethoven's Ninth Symphony, in which my father sang the tenor part. After that came the dedication speech by His Apostolic Majesty, Emperor Franz Josef I.

The venerable old monarch stood in the center of the stage and read in a slow and halting monotone.

Next to him stood Cardinal Nagel, the highest Catholic cleric in Austria. Behind the emperor, in a semicircle twelve rows deep and pressing against the wall, stood the archdukes and their archduchesses, the members of the imperial house, ministers and diplomats, officials of state and the high military. All were resplendent in their gala uniforms, with gold braid and decorations, orders and plumed hats.

My parents stood with my sister and me in the last row. Papa, having the title "Kammersänger to His Majesty's Imperial Court," ranked the same as a general and was therefore permitted on the platform.

Mama was bathed in moiré and lace and wore a wide hat with ostrich feathers. I had on my first long pants, a white suit, and was constantly admonished not to get it dirty.

Papa towered over everybody like a man on stilts and had a fine view. But *I* could see nothing. Nothing but shoes, legs, skirts, and above them various promontories of assorted male and female fannies. I heard a voice talking and asked who it was:

"It's the emperor," said Papa, "and be quiet." I tried to move around, to find some way to see what was going on, but I was pulled back and Mama hissed: "Don't fidget! Stay where you are."

She shouldn't have said that, because that set the IBM machine in motion. Somehow I loosened her grip and was gone. Irrevocably gone. Edging my way through a thick forest of pants and bustles, nudging calves and thighs, crawling and slipping like a weasel past tasseled sabers and coattails, brushing against caraculs and shakos, I emerged and found myself to the left of an imposing figure dressed in a long scarlet robe and behind an old gentleman who wore black trousers, bordered with a wide gold stripe, a white tunic with a gold collar and his breast full of decorations. He had side whiskers and read from a piece of paper. His hands trembled a little and I wondered if he was scared or so very old.

Then I suddenly recognized him: it was our emperor.

The figure in the long scarlet robe looked down at me in great surprise and halted my further advance by grabbing me firmly and planting me in front of him, with both his hands resting on my shoulders.

I felt happy and secure. I had accomplished my goal, I could see what was going on and I could hear what the emperor was saying. Not that I understood it.

Then I looked out into the auditorium, tightly packed with thousands of overdressed people, immobile in their obedient reverence.

"So that is what my father sees when he performs on a stage," I thought.

It would be easy to mention here that at this very moment in my childish breast a burning desire awoke and a resolution was made that someday I too would be standing on such a stage, looking down at the hushed multitudes, holding them in rapt silence.

But that would be a base falsehood, a gross lie. And I never lie unless it is absolutely necessary. Or convenient.

I just stood there and enjoyed the spectacle. I did wonder who the man in the scarlet robe was, but I was so used to people wearing costumes on-stage that it didn't seem strange.

I looked down into the auditorium and saw the director of the Imperial Opera, the great Gustav Mahler, sitting there with his blond wife. I knew him from rehearsals, which I was sometimes allowed to attend (hidden in a quiet corner of the opera house). He also had been to our house, but when he came, we children were quickly passed around like a tray of scarce hors d'oeuvres and sent to the exile of our playroom. We were told that Gustav Mahler was very high-strung and that children made him nervous.

I could only wish that some of my friends today would show me the same consideration that my parents showed Gustav Mahler: I also am high-strung.

The emperor finished his speech and turned in my direction. His cold blue eyes gave me a fishy stare, completely uninterested in my unexplained presence. The national anthem was sung and he left, followed by the archdukes and the archduchesses, the members of the imperial house, ministers and diplomats, officials of state and the high military, with gold braid and orders, decorations and plumed hats.

The scarlet robe leaned down to me and asked me my name. I told him. Just then Papa rushed up, trailed by Mama with ostrich feather swinging; both bowed deeply and Mama kissed the scarlet-robed man's ring. They babbled how embarrassed they were and apologized, but he laughed, patted my head and said that I was a *"neugieriger kleiner Lausbub,"* and left.

This time the "curious little rascal" was not punished, but was told that he should remember, all his life, that he was standing three feet away from the Emperor of Austria and had been held in protective custody by His Eminence, Cardinal Nagel.

Papa told me about several occasions when he was received in audience with His Majesty during his tenure at the Vienna Court Opera. Every time an honor was bestowed on him, he had to put on his court uniform, which was taken out of moth balls for the occasion, and a tailor was called in to let out more seams. He then high-tailed it to the Hofburg. At such audiences the strictest Spanish court ceremonial was religiously observed.

Of all the reigning monarchs of the twentieth century the old Emperor Franz Josef was the most reserved, the most distant.

You were not permitted to speak in his presence unless he addressed you first. And you had to answer his questions quickly and to the point. No jokes and no showing of humor were permitted, because the venerable old gentleman wouldn't have understood it anyway. After he had nodded his dismissal, you had to back out of the room, so as not to show your derrière to the imperial presence, and Papa often told me of his constant fear that he would bump into furniture or miss the door.

I remember how strange it was for me to see the pretender to the throne of Austria, Otto von Hapsburg, sitting beside me on a Fifth Avenue bus in New York during the Second World War, and I cherish the remark of a former Viennese furrier who was presented in Hollywood to Otto von Hapsburg during a reception and said jovially:

"Herrn Grosspapa hab ich gut gekannt [Your grandaddy, I knew him well.]"

On some occasions, Papa loved to play "Father" and take my sister and me to the Prater, the famous amusement park of Vienna. Mama and my grandmother didn't like these solo excursions. They felt Papa was not the perfect nursemaid for a four- and a five-year-old, but, as always, he got his way: sometimes by using the thunderbolts of the domestic tyrant, but more often by being sly. He would pick the nurse's day off and say to Grandmother:

"Mutterl, what happened to your hair?" *"Mutterl"* would

rush to the nearest mirror. "Why, what's wrong with it?" She was very easily excited.

"Wrong? *Nothing* is wrong with it. It just seems to be getting a little gray—especially around the roots, but if *you* like it that way, I guess it's all right."

For the rest of the day, Grandmother would sit in front of her dressing table, a towel around her shoulders, and with the help of a small brush dipped in a dark liquid, would stroke herself back into a natural brunette.

Next, he went to work on Mama:

"Liesi, mein Liebling, you look so pale, so tired, so exhausted." Ten minutes later, Liesi, his *Liebling,* was truly convinced that she was pale and needed rest, and he magnanimously volunteered to take the children off her hands for the rest of the afternoon.

Josef, our coachman, was summoned, and Papa settled in our open landau, his huge arms around little Gretel and small me, overflowing with well-being and satisfaction. Everybody recognized him, and he returned all greetings as gracious acknowledgment of a well-deserved tribute.

In the Prater, he was instantly surrounded by a crowd of admirers who moved along with us as we visited the different attractions. Our first stop was always at an ice-cream parlor, where we gulped cake and strawberry soda. Then we went on the roller coaster, where we usually lost the cake and strawberry soda. After the cleaning-up job, which Papa supervised—the actual work was done by the admirers—we moved on to the giant wheel, then to the Magic Grotto, where skeletons jumped up at you and ghosts appeared out of nowhere to scare you. One of Papa's favorite attractions was the shooting gallery: "And what is Herr Kammersaenger shooting at?" the proprietor would ask. "The tiger!" said Papa. "Ah, the tiger," repeated the proprietor in a voice loud enough to be heard in the back of the tent. Then Papa shot at some other target, but the tiger would fall, and the crowd cheered. Papa always got a prize which I had to carry.

Once he took us to an exhibit, the "Lady Without an Abdomen." That charming maiden's lower anatomy had been rendered invisible with the help of some trick mirrors which gave her the appearance of sitting on her navel. We were so fascinated we didn't want to move on. So Papa left us in her care and visited some other side shows, "For Adults Only." We plied the lady with questions until she took us into her confidence and showed us how the mirrors worked. We ill repaid her for her kindness; very excitedly we explained her secret to all newcomers and ignored her frantic request that we either shut up or move on.

The attraction that we loved most was Punchy Monkey. That was a man-sized robot with a face made of well-padded leather. For the equivalent of a nickel, you could hit him in the jaw. A scale would register the volume of strength expended, and Punchy Monkey would emit a growling sound, which, by its intensity, indicated the amount of pain he supposedly suffered. It was a wonderful way to give vent to one's feelings of hostility.

Papa often played Punchy Monkey with us at home. He would close his eyes, blow up his cheeks, and we would gently hit his face. He would then growl. One morning, he was still in bed and asleep. We walked in, and Gretel heard him snore. She walked up to him and let him have it, a straight right to the jaw. He jumped with pain, furious: she got terribly scared, bawled, and said: "I thought you were playing Punchy Monkey."

Later we had dinner at the Restaurant Eisvogel, which boasted a sixteen-piece lady orchestra. Papa ordered for us. All the things *he* liked best: highly seasoned goulash and very strong Quargel (a high-potency Limburger) with caraway seed. He also let us nip from his beer—"Milk you can get at home," he said—and we arrived long past our bedtime, clothes dirty, dead tired, stomachs upset, and exceedingly happy.

2.

IN 1909 WE ALL TOOK OUR FIRST trip to America. Papa had been engaged to sing at the Metropolitan Opera in New York and his contract stipulated that he was to be paid transportation for his entire entourage.

The entourage consisted of Mama, my sister, and myself;

Fräulein Wilhelmine Weiss, our governess, nicknamed Wuschti;

Frieda, my mother's personal maid and general factotum;

Mitzi Hatchicheck, our Czechoslovak cook;

Oscar Dachs, my father's piano accompanist, and Mrs. Dachs;

Dixi and Puppi, our two Maltese terriers;

Kiki, our black cat, who was pregnant. But we didn't know that until she gave birth to nine kittens on the high seas;

Piep, our canary bird, also known as "Herr Kammersaenger" because he sang so beautifully;

Laura the parrot.

And my frog! (I'm sure that he also had a name, but I've forgotten it.)

"Packing" started a whole week before the journey. Because no wardrobe department of any opera house anywhere had clothes to fit the gigantic measurements of my father, he always carried his own costumes. They were very beautiful, especially designed and fashioned for him in Paris, and represented a big investment. Their care and their packing and unpacking were Mama's domain.

Every garment, from tights to suits of armor, was carefully wrapped in tissue paper and the semiprecious stones were protected with cotton and wool cloth. For every role he sang, there was a special trunk. They were all marked: "Otello," "Tannhäuser," "Lohengrin," "Aïda," etc. A special long casket-like trunk contained the sword, lances, daggers, scimitars; a large valise was for make-up, wigs, beards, and the stage jewelry.

Whenever we crossed a border, and in Europe that could happen every eight hours if you had a fast train, there was the tedious customs inspection. Most of the time, the customs men were nice, but sometimes you drew a real stinker who made poor Mama unpack every piece. Needless to say he didn't help her repack it.

As all these baggage inspections usually took place in some drafty hall, Papa could not be present, because he lived in constant fear of catching cold and damaging his voice.

Before we set out on a trip, Papa called us all into his room and we said a prayer. Then each took up his personal luggage. Everyone had to carry his share.

Papa had a large brown bag, sort of a carpetbag, which was called *"Die Wurmbrandt Tasche."* Why it was so called I don't know, probably the name of the manufacturer.

Die Wurmbrandt Tasche played an important part in all our travels. Papa could never close it; he always complained that it was too small and that—by God—someday he would get a larger one. He never did.

Into it Papa packed a complete desk set. Blotters, trays for pens and pencils, an inkwell, a bottle of ink, his clock, and a compass. Why he carried a compass we were never able to find out. The bag also contained most of his photographic equipment: two stereo cameras, a tripod, boxes of photographic glass plates, dark slides, and a bag with a white powder he used to make flash exposures. That of course involved taking along another tripod with a tray at the top on which the powder was poured before it was ignited. After every picture thus taken, the whole room was filled with acid-smelling smoke, and it took an hour until we were able to recognize each other again. All photos from this period showed both my sister and me with tightly closed eyes, because we were waiting for the flash. And we were always accused of ruining his pictures, which indeed we did.

The bag also held his diary and a large black hard-cover book into which he wrote down every penny spent. And a whole portable pharmacy: nose sprays, throat sprays, pills, medicines, several kinds of vaporizers and inhalators, all neatly labeled. An alcohol burner to produce steam for the inhalator, the alcohol for the burner, several books, leather frames with photos of the entire family and all the pets. An assortment of hand tools, screwdrivers, drill, little hammers, and a long carborundum sharpening stone.

In one of his breast pockets Papa carried a large leather folder which held the tickets and passports for the whole family, including governess, maid, cook, and his piano accompanist, Oscar Dachs. He lived in mortal fear that somebody might lose a passport or the ticket and thereby delay a concert or an opera performance.

In the other breast pocket was a wallet which contained money, with a special billfold for the currency of whatever country we passed or landed in. All through the trip Papa tapped his breast pockets every few minutes, to make sure that all was still there. I could never understand why he was so nervous about traveling, as he spent half his life on trains and boats.

Punctuality was a fetish with him. When we went to a theater, he was usually there to greet the ushers when they arrived, and if the gate at a railroad station was already opened when he arrived, he spoke darkly about nearly missing the train.

Mama was the keeper of all the keys. Everything was locked, every key had a label which told to which bag or trunk it belonged. This satchel was heavy, but Mama held onto it.

My sister carried the cage with the canary bird.

And I had to carry a Pompadour bag; and in it was the *pot de chambre.*

It was all part of an elaborate plan to protect our health. Whenever we went to a restaurant, boiling hot water was ordered and all knives, forks, and spoons were meticulously cleaned. The edge of every glass was wiped before we were allowed to use it. And whenever we had to go to the bathroom, we were forced to use that abominable potty.

I deeply resented the indignity of having to carry that loathsome receptacle and refused to believe that it looked like a *bonbonnière,* which was what my parents constantly assured me. After I had dropped and broken two of them, they bought one made of enamel. But that one chipped and was rated dangerous.

We traveled with thirty-one large steamer trunks and about forty smaller pieces of luggage. The departure from our apartment in Vienna was a highly entertaining spectacle. A huge flat wagon was hired to carry all our trunks and baggage to the Westbahnhof, all, that is, except a few handbags too precious to be trusted to a porter.

Mama and Frieda stood on the street and supervised the loading, Papa stood by a window on the first floor and supervised the supervising. He was very concerned that all should be securely tied to the wagon so nothing would get lost in the wild gallop to the railway station.

Traffic in front of our building all but stopped. A policeman had to clear the sidewalk of curious passers-by and of devoted fans of my father who had assembled for a farewell demonstration. When all was loaded and ready to leave, the first crisis arose: Frieda refused to ride next to the coachman on the box. She claimed it was undignified and unbecoming her status as a personal maid.

The argument was relayed to my father: outraged at such mutiny, he stepped out onto the balcony and ordered her in great, full-ringing tones, to get the hell on that box and stop being a prima donna. As he appeared on the balcony, the crowd below broke into applause, but he was too furious to acknowledge it.

Frieda heard her master's voice and quickly scrambled up onto the box, holding on her lap a straw basket which contained Kiki the cat. The driver let out a loud "Hueaah!" and the first load left. Next pulled up three one-horse carriages. Into the first were stuffed Fräulein Weiss and Mitzi Hatchicheck, and the air space around them was filled with every imaginable piece of luggage. Fräulein Weiss carried Laura, the parrot, his cage hidden in a canvas bag with air holes.

I was standing by the window next to Papa and saw that Mitzi was crossing herself just as the carriage moved on. Having heard and read much about Indians, scalpings, and the stake of torture, I began to feel a little apprehensive about the journey.

The next carriage contained Oscar Dachs and *Frau*, who were considerably miffed because Papa had insisted that they come to our building first instead of going directly to the station. But good Oscar had a habit of being late and Papa didn't want to go through the agony of having to wait for him until he arrived at the very last moment when the train nearly pulled out.

Some more baggage was added to their luggage, which added to their miff, and when their carriage departed, a considerable amount of frost showed on their sunny faces.

Last pulled up Josef, our personal coachman. He got off the box and made sure that all the windows were closed; he arranged the blanket, and with a great, sweeping gesture reminiscent of the acting style of Molière, he gave the "ready" signal up to the balcony. An expectant murmur rippled through the crowd which pressed against the front door. There was a short wait, and then Papa crashed through—in heavy fur coat, a shawl wrapped around his neck and holding a handkerchief in front of his face to ward off possible drafts. The footboard of the carriage bent down low as if in greeting when he stepped on it, and after he had settled himself inside the whole carriage was six inches closer to the ground.

The crowd cheered and an ill-advised fan stepped up to ask for an autograph. "Are you insane?" Papa roared. "NOW?"

The fan fled.

Next came Mama, waving good-by to my grandmother, then my sister and I squeezed ourselves in. There was never enough room for our feet, what with Papa's huge legs and Mama's voluminous skirts. My sister held the cage with the canary bird and I held the Pompadour bag with the hateful potty inside and gripped a glass jar which held my frog. The carriage jerked, the crowd cheered, wished us a good journey, yelled, *"Hoch Slezak!"* and some of the younger fans ran along with us for a while.

Mama started to mention a few of the things that she had forgotten to tell Grandmother, whose mission it was to close up the apartment while we were gone. After riding a few blocks Papa let out a choked cry of anguish:

"My God, the passports!"

He started to feel all his pockets in feverish haste and suddenly declared that he remembered distinctly that he had given them to Mama.

She denied it—he was positive—Mama was equally positive and a frantic guessing game began where they could have been left. Very reluctantly the carriage was stopped and ordered to return. (That was supposed to spell bad luck.) Papa kept on searching in all the folds of his clothes and with a sigh of relief announced that he had found them. The driver turned around again and pointed his horse toward the station.

My sister announced darkly that she might get carsick any moment. She was COMMANDED not to DARE do such a thing, and a lively discussion arose if it would be wise to open one of the windows just one little bit, but the fear of Papa catching cold got the upper hand and Gretel bravely held back till we got out at the station.

Only then did she let go.

Wuschti took charge of her and Papa and I hurried ahead to our compartment, Mama counted and re-counted the luggage.

And then came that repetitious game of paying the porters. That game is particular to Vienna. In no other city in Europe, except maybe in the Balkans or in the Orient, is there such haggling. Vienna has no fixed rates for carrying baggage. When you ask a porter how much you owe him, he starts calling you Herr Baron and trusts that whatever you consider proper will be all right with him. This puts you on the defensive and usually leads to overtipping. But any sum of money you hand him, regardless of the amount, brings forth cries of outrage and anguish.

He begins by telling you how much he has to pay for goulash; he tells you the price of a liter of beer and a liter of wine; of the rising cost of tobacco; and lets you know how he is suffering under the horrible heat of the day (if the transaction takes place during the winter, it's the unbearable cold). He tries to move your heart with recalling all the afflictions his family is suffering from and how much the doctors cost.

You have to have very strong moral fiber not to be ruffled by such a loud public exhibition and to be able to walk away in dignified silence, disregarding the insults and ill wishes that are heaped upon you.

The first thing Papa always did when he entered a train compartment was to produce a sign: "RESERVIERT."

He hated to share a drawing room with other passengers. When we all traveled together, it wasn't important, because we filled the compartment anyway, but when he and Mama traveled alone, it took some doing to discourage others from joining them.

On the door of the train compartment there was usually attached a metal frame, with sliding numbers corresponding to the seats inside the compartment. These numbers were pushed to the right, when the seat was taken, and to the left when it was available. It could be operated only with a key, which was in the possession of the conductor. But Papa had one of these keys and, quick as a magician, he put all the numbers on "reserved." Usually that was enough to discourage would-be fellow travelers. And a tip usually took care of the conductor.

For extremely overcrowded trains Papa carried in his *Wurmbrandt Tasche* a sign, decorated with red crosses, which spelled: "HOSPITAL COMPARTMENT." This he hung outside the door and closed the curtains. Nobody ever entered.

Next he produced the *Perolin Spritze*. That was a long chrome spray gun, the type used in movie houses to purify the air. You pointed it downward, pulled the handle toward you and exhaled it upward. After a few strokes a fine mist of pine-scented fluid settled over everything and the air was considered pure.

As my mother didn't mind riding backward on trains, she always took the window seat opposite Papa. Then Papa put on a pair of slippers, slipped into an alpaca jacket, and settled down to travel.

I fed my frog worms, but he wouldn't eat; everybody in our party checked in and reported that all was well, Frieda no longer felt undignified and the frost had melted off the Oscar Dachses.

The porter made up our beds while we all went to the dining car. Later we were tucked in, and the night swallowed our train—rushing, bumping, and rattling ahead.

Of course, in the middle of the night, when first we crossed the German border at Salzburg, and later in the day, the French border at Strasbourg, customs inspectors and passport scrutinizers, deadly serious and inflated by their importance, invaded our compartment. Everything was inspected: questions were asked, forms were filled out, at least ten pieces of luggage had to be opened and partially unpacked (usually the ones that were hardest to repack), and in the end a bribe was reluctantly given by my father to avoid further annoyance.

Frugality rather than moral considerations was the basis for his reluctance.

In Paris our whole caravan descended upon a hotel for a night's stay. French hotels never seemed partial to dogs and cats, so our small menagerie was smuggled in, hidden in their various camouflaged containers. There were always anxious and apprehensive moments until we were past the reception clerks and the elevator man, lest a bark or a miaow, a cheep, or the nasal voice of our parrot, announcing that he was a dear bird, should betray that we harbored four-legged and winged stowaways.

Our quadrupeds had been pan-trained. Two large pastry pans strewn with sand (we carried ten kilos with us) were placed in the bathroom and in relays our dogs and the cat were cajoled and encouraged to perform their natural functions, and when everything was finally done, an elaborate show of completely undeserved appreciation and praise was acted out. The two Maltese dogs had very long silky hair, and after such performances quite often the necessity arose to give them a hip bath.

The next morning we boarded the boat train for Cherbourg, where our steamer, *Kronprinzessin Caecilie,* was lying at anchor outside the harbor. The same procedure of counting and re-counting the luggage took place, and after we got off the train we had to walk about four hundred feet along the quay to board the tender that was to take us out to the steamer.

The quay was narrow and everybody pushed and shoved to be the first on board; and in the pushing and shoving, I dropped the Pompadour bag with the hateful potty. It was a new one made of porcelain, a farewell gift of a well-meaning aunt, and when it broke it made a lovely sound. Mama let out an anguished scream, as if I had damaged the Holy Grail. Her screams scared me and I dropped the glass with my frog. It also broke.

The frog realized that this was his chance to get away (I have a suspicion that he was never really happy in that jar, sitting on that silly ladder), and *away* he got—with long, big jumps. Papa shouted at me to let that god-damn frog go and to pick up the *bonbonnière* bag with the broken crockery.

But that was clearly an ORDER. Remember!

So off *I* was, dashing through stomping legs and between swinging valises in frantic pursuit of my frog. A few times I thought I had him, but he was as slippery as a frog ought to be, and just as I reached out for the final catch, the foot of an elaborately gowned, large lady came down on him.

I yelled, *"Attention, ma grenouille!"*—but it was too late. She slipped, slithered, let out a yell and executed a beautiful prattfall. Realizing that my *grenouille* was harmed beyond repair, I threw a screaming tantrum in which the lady, who was still lying on the quay and blocking traffic, joined me.

Her wrath and that of all the slowed-down *voyageurs* was heaped on me and especially on Papa—probably for having fathered me. But he, to my great surprise, stood by me and became my defender instead of doing the sensible thing: walking away and pretending he'd never seen me before in his life.

When we got to the tender, without frog and without Pompadour bag, I was still bawling, but nobody paid any attention to me. The worry about counting the luggage, about Papa catching cold, and about one of our party falling off the gangplank into the sea made everyone ignore my grief.

After we were settled in our cabin, I went to the purser and asked him if PERHAPS, by CHANCE, they HAPPENED to have a frog on board. He laughed gaily and said:

"Just the legs, my little one, and if you're a good boy, you may eat some for dinner."

For the rest of my life I've never been able to enjoy frog's legs.

The first evening on board was truly memorable. We all dressed for dinner, and it was the first time in my life that I was allowed to choose from the menu what *I* wanted, instead of being told what I will have. Many of the regular singers of the Metropolitan Opera were on board returning from their vacation. The great Caruso, Antonio Scotti, Emmy Destinn, Lucie Weidt, Alfred Soomer, and many more. After dinner Oscar Dachs played the piano in the salon and the evening turned into a nice, warm impromptu *Singfest.*

Papa, of course, had heard Caruso's voice on recordings, but he was dying to hear him in real life. Later, after Papa and Caruso had become good friends, Caruso told Papa how curious *he* had been to hear the voice of the man he knew would become his rival at the Met. So the two greatest tenors of their time actually auditioned for each other and the evening was full of praise, backslapping, and exaggerated camaraderie.

In 1912 Caruso made a wonderful caricature: small, dapper Caruso looking up angrily at Slezak's huge, shapeless form, glaring down on his rival. He called it "Perfect Harmony."

But the month of the year was November, and once we got out of the English Channel, the Atlantic Ocean showed its grimmest face. Came morning and Mama was flat on her back, unable to move except to ring for the stewardess. Papa was equally sick, and described his condition as "gorgonzola green, defenseless, and weary of life."

Frieda and Mitzi Hatchicheck were prostrate with *mal de mer,* and also our good governess Wuschti Weiss was unable to govern. So my sister and I had a glorious trip, roaming all over the boat at will, eating alone at our big table in the dining room. Every few hours, we put in a dutiful appearance at the bed of sorrow of our parents, who just lay there, groaning feebly and imploring us in all but inaudible whispers please not to fall overboard.

I struck up a friendship with a fellow passenger named Marconi. He gave me my first autograph. Of course, I asked him for it, not because I knew who he was or what it was he had invented, but only because everybody else asked him to sign his name. Enrico Caruso made a sketch of me and promised me that he would personally give me singing lessons, should I ever decide to become a tenor.

The first to come up for air after five days of rolling and heaving seas was Papa. His face was the color of pale bacon, he staggered on deck and plunked into the next chair, where a steward propped him up with pillows and wrapped him in blankets like a mummy.

The captain walked by and Papa reproached him severely for the way in which he sailed his ship. He complained bitterly about his miserable days of suffering, volunteered his opinion of what he thought of the good ship *Kronprinzessin Caecilie,* and also suggested what the North German Lloyd could do with her. The captain laughed and allowed that Papa had such an amusing way of expressing himself. He assured him that the trip was not really a bad one—as some trips are—that it was just a slight sea, the tail end of a heavy storm which he had successfully circumnavigated. Papa looked out over the ocean.

"Way back in the distance," he asked, "is that land?"

"No," said the captain. "That's the horizon."

"Better than nothing," replied Papa, and sank back into his pillows.

But even during his greatest misery, he didn't lose his sense of humor: when the going was roughest, he sent the steward to Cabin 412, where Professor Dachs and *Frau* were laid up on their bunks, with a message that "Herr Kammersaenger was expecting him in the music salon to study." The steward reported back that he could not get a definite reply out of Professor Dachs, but, judging from his groans and prolonged moaning, he didn't think that the professor would be able to come to the salon. Papa sent several more messengers with the same call to work to Cabin 412. The last one returned and complained that Professor Dachs had thrown an ash tray at him and used language unbecoming a professor.

Then came the great day of arrival in New York. Mama didn't get out of bed until the Statue of Liberty was in sight, and very wisely stuck to that routine on all following ocean crossings. As we steamed up the harbor, the health inspectors and newspaper reporters came on board. With them was a publicity agent whom Papa had been advised to hire. That good man—his name was Jack—was a drumbeater with a flair for the theatrical. While coming up the gangplank he noticed a passenger in steerage who had with him a goat. He quickly rented that goat for an hour, and when the reporters came on deck for the traditional shipboard interview, there was the goat, standing next to my father.

Papa, at that point, didn't speak English well enough to understand all that was said, and Mama, who spoke it fluently, wasn't present. So Jack did all the talking. Many pictures were taken, the reporters laughed a lot and departed.

We disembarked, and the whole party, with the exception of Mama and Frieda, was off to the Hotel Ansonia, where a large apartment awaited us.

Poor Mama had to go through the long and tedious procedure of clearing the entire luggage through customs. Every bag, suitcase, and theatrical costume trunk had to be completely unpacked. Some of the helmets, swords, and breastplates of Papa's costumes were studded with jewels. They aroused the suspicion of the customs inspectors and a jewelry appraiser was called in to make sure that we didn't try to smuggle in real diamonds, emeralds, and sapphires under the guise of costume jewelry. The second-act costume of *Aïda* alone had about three hundred stones embroidered to its armor. The shield of the first act of Lohengrin had seventy-eight—every stone was scrutinized and it took over nine hours to clear everything. The theatrical trunks were shipped to the Met and Mama and Frieda arrived late in the evening with the rest of the luggage at the hotel. There they found Papa raging and roaring.

The evening papers had hit the streets and announced in great headlines that Leo Slezak, the giant Czech tenor, never sang without his pet goat tethered in his dressing room; that just before he went on-stage, he always bent down forward and encouraged the goat to butt him in the behind because he considered that good luck, that he personally milked the goat twice a day but never drank the milk, just used it as a gargle. They told what the goat ate, that her name was Dinorah and how difficult it was to keep her in a hotel. They further proclaimed that Slezak always walked around barefoot because he considered that good for his voice, and how it pained him to have to wear shoes when on the opera or concert stage; that he used to be a wrestler and would accept all challenges.

My parents were horrified by such undignified publicity, and Jack was fired the same evening. Later we found that he also worked for Barnum and Bailey.

The whole thing backfired a few months later, when a wrestler challenged Papa to a match and when many people, while he was on a concert tour, expressed keen disappointment that Dinorah was not traveling with him, and that he was never seen barefoot.

A few years later, Papa told the story of having been suspected of trying to smuggle real jewels under the guise of costume jewelry to a very well-known Austrian actor, Alfred Gerasch. In 1918, after the monarchy was overthrown, Alfred Gerasch, who was loyal to the emperor, arranged for a series of guest appearances in Switzerland. He is supposed to have taken out of Austria all of the immensely valuable collection of jewels belonging to the imperial house of the Hapsburgs by having them embroidered on his costumes.

A few days after our arrival, after all was unpacked, our life settled down to normal. The cook complained about everything in the kitchen, the flour, the eggs, the taste of butter, and the range. But within a few days, she made a complete about-face, became enthusiastically pro-American, started to forget her language, and mixed the few English words she had picked up into the conversation. She also thought that "Mitzi" Hatchicheck sounded too foreign and insisted on being called "Mary" Hatchicheck. Not wanting to retard the process of assimilation and upset the melting pot, we, of course, complied.

Papa didn't trust automobiles, so he rented a carriage. It was maroon-colored, heavily upholstered, badly ventilated, and smelled musty. The fact that Papa never opened the windows—colds, you remember—didn't improve the atmosphere. There was even less room in it than in our Viennese *Einspaenner*, but it had excellent springs that made the carriage sway gently instead of rock and made *even me* carsick. It was powered by one horse, named Milada.

Communication with the coachman was achieved through a speaking tube into which we yelled or whistled to attract his attention. *Sometimes* Mischko, our Bohemian charioteer, heard our signals and responded. Then we were in trouble. His English was completely unintelligible, and only Papa, speaking to him in Czech, was able to make himself understood.

The day our good Lord passed out brains, Mischko must have been absent. He was a well of gentle stupidity. It took him a full week to learn the way from the Ansonia Hotel, at Seventy-third Street and Broadway to the Metropolitan Opera House at Fortieth Street and Broadway, without getting lost. He was always looking for short cuts and ended up near the Hudson or the East River. When told to wait at the stage entrance at the Met on 39th Street to drive my father back to the hotel, it was a safe bet that he would be waiting patiently and conscientiously at the front door of the Ansonia Hotel. When Mama went shopping without Papa it was always disaster. After letting her out at whatever store she patronized, he would disappear and she spent more time searching for the carriage in side streets than in the shops.

He was fired three times a day and stayed on for four years partly because he was such a pleasant and lovable idiot and mainly because Papa was touched that he was so good to his horse. He loved and worshiped Milada. When the weather was really bad, with snow and rain being whipped through the canyons of New York by a forty-mile-an-hour wind, Mischko always reported sick and sent a substitute. Of course he wasn't sick at all, but didn't want to subject his beloved horse to the unpleasantness of the elements.

He told us that he often fed her *knedlitschki*—Bohemian

dumplings—to reward her for some extracurricular good deed; judging from her explosive exhaust and backfirings, we could well believe it.

The corridors of the Ansonia Hotel became our indoor playground, raceway, and ball park. For outdoor activities there was glorious Central Park with a lake, with rocks and caves and various hiding places where we saw imaginary Indians lurking around the bushes and where we looked for gold nuggets and rattlesnakes, also imaginary.

On November 17 I was allowed to go to the Metropolitan Opera for the debut of my father. The opera was *Otello,* and I was briefed again that whatever I saw on the stage was only make-believe and that, when Papa as Otello strangles Desdemona and stabs himself, he doesn't really kill her and for the stabbing uses a rubber knife. Frances Alda, Gatti-Casazza's wife, sang Desdemona, Antonio Scotti was Iago, and Arturo Toscanini conducted.

After Otello informs Desdemona that he will kill her, she runs to the door, which is locked. Papa as Otello picked her up by the waist, lifted her high above his head, and carried her in long, slow strides across the huge stage of the Metropolitan to her inevitable doom, lowered her on the bed, and suffocated her with the pillow.

An unbelieving gasp went through the audience. This athletic feat impressed the dowagers in the diamond circle as much as his singing. That night he was a tremendous success.

The next time I was permitted to go to the Met was to hear Mozart's *Magic Flute.* That's a very difficult opera to explain to a child—or to a grownup at that—and the briefing I got was perfunctory. All I was really interested in was that there would be a snake chasing Tamino when he made his first entrance, and whether or not Papageno had live birds in his cage. When Papa came running on-stage, singing:

> *"Zu Huelfe, zu Huelfe, sonst bin ich verloren,*
> *Der listigen Schlange zum Opfer erkoren . . ."*

I got panicky, jumped up from my seat, and yelled at the top of my voice: "Watch out, Papa, there is a snake."

People laughed and I was quickly evicted by Mama and told to consider myself disgraced.

That was the first time I raised my voice in the Metropolitan Opera. Little did I know that fifty years later I would be standing on that stage, this time being *paid* for raising my voice and occupying the same dressing room my father had then occupied. And it is comforting to note that, except for a little superficial dusting, no alterations or redecorating had been done to that room since 1909.

Actually I had made my operatic debut many many years earlier, as Lohengrin.

At the Cologne Opera House, where Papa was then singing, the arrival of the noble knight from Monsalvat, standing proudly in the swan-drawn boat in his silvery armor, was staged in perspective that must have been quite startling: at the farthest depth of the stage first appeared a tiny boat with a tiny Lohengrin in it, and it was moved across the stage. A while later a somewhat larger boat with a somewhat larger Lohengrin could be seen, and finally Papa, as the real Lohengrin, was pulled in sight.

Well, at one performance the tiny Lohengrin was I. With great secrecy, as a surprise for Mama, I was smuggled into the opera house, dressed, and bearded. I was four years old, didn't cry, so I must have enjoyed it. The joke fizzled out because Mama, from her box, never recognized that it was her own flesh and blood who was standing in the boat. Only when I was brought to Papa's dressing room after the first act did she point an accusing finger at him: "Why isn't that child in bed?"

Papa, who had sung for eight years under the strict artistic discipline of Gustav Mahler, was happy to find in Arturo Toscanini a taskmaster who was just as exacting in his demands and who tolerated no sloppiness. Of course, he could be a holy terror if anything went wrong. Once, during a performance of *Die Meistersinger,* Papa made a small musical mistake. His dressing-room door burst open during the intermission and revealed the prompter, shaking with fear—ashen.

"*Ah, disgrazia—avete mangiato un quarto—Maestro è furibondo!*" (Ah, what a disgrace, you have swallowed a quarter note—Maestro is furious.) And then he pointed tragically into the hallway: "*Guarda!*" Papa got up and "guarded." There stood frail, small Toscanini, who banged his head against the wall, groaning: "*Questo tenore è una bestia!*" Papa bent down to him, apologized profusely for the *disgrazia,* and, properly dismayed with regret, promised that he would never never again swallow a quarter note. The maestro calmed down, looked up at Papa, who was towering over him, and murmured darkly: "*Caro, ero terribile!*" Then he added: "*Ti perdono.*" Papa said happily: "*Grazie, maestro, grazie,*" reached down, lifted him up to face level, kissed him on both cheeks, and set him down again.

Toscanini screamed and jumped up and down with uncontrolled white fury. It took Papa two weeks to get back in his good graces.

When the spring tour of the Metropolitan began, Papa was advised that it would be good publicity to hire a private railroad car. It had a dining room, a small music room furnished with an upright piano, and came equipped with a Negro porter and cook. The car was hooked onto regular trains and when we arrived at our destination was detached, pulled to a siding, and what had been a form of locomotion became an abode.

Of course, there was friction between Mary (formerly Mitzi) Hatchicheck and the colored cook, because Mary regarded the kitchen as her sole domain, and so did he. The results of this friction, which we had to eat, were not too attractive, and there were lively scenes. After about one month of this high-class gypsy life, Papa abandoned the private car as too expensive and impractical—my parents traveled on—and we children, Wuschti, the cook, and all the animals with the exception of the two Maltese terriers, were sent back to New York to the Ansonia Hotel. There we led a more normal life, but, frankly, I much preferred living on a train.

In Houston, Texas, he sang Otello. The program not only told the story of the opera, but managed to sell space for advertising as well. This is the way it read:

"OTHELLO"
Opera In Four Acts
by
Guiseppe Verdi
Act I

The people of Cypria, on their knees, are praying for the safety of Othello, whose ship is fighting the elements. The danger passes. Othello arrives and greets the people with the words:

USE CRISCO, THE BEST SHORTENING

"Rejoice! The Turk is vanquished and drowned in the sea." The people hail Othello.

CRISCO IS UNSURPASSED

Jago, jealous of Cassio, who enjoys Othello's confidence, tries to render Cassio drunk. A drinking song

CRISCO HAS NO RIVAL

is heard and Cassio, by now quite drunk, attacks Montano. Othello rushes in and calls out:

CRISCO IS ECONOMICAL

"Down with your swords!" Cassio is being demoted. Desdemona, Othello's lovely bride appears in the doorway to the castle. Othello takes her hand and they sing a lovely duet

CRISCO USERS ARE SATISFIED

which belongs to the best Verdi wrote, and is considered one of the pearls of operatic music.

Thus ends the first act and thus Crisco seeps through all four acts until in the end:

After Othello has strangled Desdemona, he plunges his dagger into his breast and, dying, he sings the touching phrase:

ASK ONLY FOR CRISCO,
THE FAMOUS SHORTENING

"Kiss me, kiss me again!" He dies. End of the opera.

"Essere un cantante in Italia è una vergogna." (To be a singer in Italy is a disgrace.) These bitter words Caruso said when Papa asked him why he refused to sing in his own country.

In the early 1900s, the life of an opera singer in Italy was a sad lot. The powerful Ricordis and Sonzognos ruled as despots. Every impresario had to submit a list of the entire cast before he got permission to perform the opera. So nearly all of the opera singers, with the exception of a few of the big stars, had to sign clauses in their contracts.

One of them was known as *"Il Protesto del Pubblico o del Maestro,"* which meant that, if the maestro for any reason did not like the singer, his contract became automatically null and void, and if the impresario wanted to get rid of him, all he had to do was to hire several rowdies in the gallery and have them "protest" with catcalls, whistles, and boos.

During Caruso's earlier years as a singer, he was engaged by an Italian impresario to sing at Barcelona. He had not yet obtained the fame of his later years, but already commanded ten thousand pesetas for a performance. After the second act of *L'Elisir d'amore,* a tumultuous demonstration began in the balcony. Yells of *"Vaya, vaya, basta"* were heard. The rest of the audience protested vigorously against such rowdiness, but the impresario came backstage pretending to be heartbroken. *"Carissimo Caruso, mi dispiace tanto* . . . I am so terribly sorry, but the audience is protesting, and I am thus forced to cancel your contract, but as I am afraid this would hurt your career, I am willing to keep you on but only at two thousand pesetas per performance." Caruso got up, punched the impresario in the nose, left the theater, went back to his hotel, packed his bags, and left town.

The same thing happened to the famous Zenatello at the Teatro Colón. He had been signed for thirty performances at fourteen thousand pesetas per show. His debut was *Aïda,* and after the aria "Celeste Aïda," the well-arranged *"Il Protesto del Pubblico"* began. Again the impresario came backstage and made the same little speech, the identical offer he had made to Caruso in Rome. But Zenatello just smiled, *"Carissimo amico,* you should have read my contract more carefully before you went to the expense and trouble to arrange *'Il Protesto del Pubblico,'* because then you would have noticed that I scratched out that shameful paragraph before I signed." He stayed on for his thirty performances.

Opera is part of the Italians' life, and they attend it

with the same enthusiasm and lack of reverence that is found with baseball games in America. Sometimes they are in a kidding mood, talk back to the singer, and voice their disapproval. At a performance of *I Pagliacci* in Naples, the baritone sang the prologue. The audience didn't like him and yelled, stomped, and whistled. Suddenly, the poor devil, who was probably hungry, stepped down to the footlights and called out: *"Perche fischiate a me—Aspettate il tenore."* (Why are you whistling at me. Just wait until the tenor comes.) In the second act, after Nedda had finished her aria—she had sung it badly and off pitch—there broke out wild applause from the gallery and calls of *"Bis."* They wouldn't stop until she repeated the aria, and then they forced her to sing it a third time. When the customers in the orchestra protested, a voice from the gallery yelled: *"Deve cantarlo fina che lo conosce."* (She must sing it until she knows it.)

The last time Caruso appeared in Italy, he donated his services for four benefit performances for flood relief. During his last performance, one of his high notes broke, and the public started booing him. Caruso was so outraged that he yelled at them: *"Voi siete dei porci."* (You are pigs.) A police escort had to take him out of the theater to protect him against a lynching mob.

3.

I DON'T KNOW WHAT CAUSED ME to become such a well-educated, erudite, lovable, nay adorable human being (when that gratifying feeling of self-adulation becomes too strong, I lie down for a while, and it usually goes away by itself). But it most certainly was not caused by my early schooling and the smattering of education that drifted my way.

Until I was eleven years old, I was a tutored child in transit. I was fed knowledge and wisdom on the run, like a channel swimmer who is handed nourishment from the accompanying boat while he comes up for air between strokes.

The Austrian public school system furnished the curriculum, laid out in progressive steps, and Wuschti, our governess and duenna, was the supervising schoolmarm.

Papa's various piano accompanists became my gurus. (That's Indian for "teacher"; I found the word in Roget's Thesaurus and I am showing off.)

The gurus were chosen, not only for their pleasant personality, cleanliness, musicianship, and virtuosity at the piano, but equally with an eye toward their scholastic abilities. Hotel rooms, hotel lobbies, restaurants, trains to and from Paris, Milano, Vienna, London, New York, Chicago—or wherever Papa's career took us—became my schoolrooms. But whenever Papa needed the guru, my lessons were abruptly interrupted. This nomadic form of schooling held many advantages for me: I saw a good deal of the world at an early age and managed to absorb, without the pain of study, several languages.

In June, when the opera season was over, we made the trip to Vienna for the yearly day of reckoning. I was taken, especially well scrubbed and impeccably dressed (to make a good impression) to the Schwarzenberg School. There I sat, in the conference room, like little Jesus in the temple, being questioned by the elders. I don't know whether it was my father's fame and popularity or the accumulation of learning that filled my well of knowledge, but every year I passed the tests and was pronounced fit to be fed heavier doses of education.

I never had the companionship of other children. My competitive spirits were completely undeveloped and I never learned discipline.

In the fall of 1913, just as we were about to embark on our yearly trip to the United States, my sister had to have an appendectomy and couldn't travel. So my parents had to leave us behind and sail alone.

It was then that I began my scholastic Odyssey. Like a little ball in a squash court is bounced off all six walls, so was I bounced off the various walls of learning. My first one-year stand I played at the Theresianum.

During the days of the Austrian monarchy the Theresianum was *the* most exclusive school in Vienna. It had been founded in 1746 by the Empress Maria Theresia as a training ground for the young members of the imperial house and the aristocracy. Even in 1913, it was very difficult to be admitted if one was not born to the nobility, but because of Papa's position as a celebrated member of His Majesty's Court Opera House, I was accepted without even having a measly little "von" in front of my name.

It was a military school: we had to wear uniforms, sword at our left, our hair cropped—seven millimeters during the winter and three millimeters during the summer. The illusion that the extra four-millimeter length in our haircut kept us comfortably warm was tenaciously adhered to. Only a few especially chosen ones, the members of the imperial house, were permitted to wear their hair long, because they sometimes had official duties at court as pages. One of these duties was to function as honor guard at the bier of whoever happened to die at court, standing next to the casket, motionless, and not allowed to look left or right, or to laugh or scratch themselves.

It was a very strict school, with a rigid discipline, that was completely alien to me. To have to get up every morning at the same time, attend regular classes in the same schoolroom, have fixed hours for homework, to be allowed just so many minutes for the morning toilet, for breakfast, for recreation—all these things that are natural to any regular schoolboy—were new and strange to me.

Twice a year we had "theatricals." There I celebrated my first "triumph" as an actor! The play was *William Tell* and I was Gessler, the cruel tyrant.

As I saw it, it was the best part, because I was allowed to make my entrance and play my big scene on horseback, with everybody else on foot. The horse I rode was a trained white Lipizzaner who high-stepped, danced, and pranced as if it were standing on a red-hot pavement.

I felt instinctively that the horse was stealing the scene from me, so I began to overact and mugg and together we managed to steal the whole show from William Tell and the poor unfortunate child who had to play his son, balancing an apple on his head. But the outcome was most wonderful: I was handed that piece of fruit in recognition of my performance. Coming from a family of professional entertainers, I of course considered that gift as a form of remuneration and shared that, my edible salary, with the horse, which I felt was partially responsible for my success. A noble gesture, indeed, and one that I have successfully managed never again to repeat during my long career.

Being high-spirited and craving the approval of my fellow students, I naturally committed many trespasses and found myself continuously in trouble.

One of my offenses was even considered serious enough to warrant "incarceration":

In the hallways of our school and in some of the classrooms, we had electric light bulbs that were exposed and pointing downward. They were pear-shaped and had a small glass tip at the end.

One Mephistofelean chum bet me ten kronen that I could not knock off thirty of these little tips without breaking some of the bulbs. I took that bet under consideration and secretly went into training in the locker room of our gym. Soon I learned that with a ruler a foot and a half long, good aim and a steady hand, a proper stance and a smooth follow-through, it was a cinch to win.

It was most exciting: the whole class made book on me, and not only did I knock off thirty tips, but nonchalantly added twenty more for good measure. I felt like a hero and with side bets and all I made fifteen kronen. And half the school was plunged into darkness.

Naturally there followed an investigation, and after horrible threats of mass reprisals against the whole student body some nasty little Benedict Arnold spoke up and put the finger on me. I was summoned to the governor's office.

First I was told the price of some sixty-odd light bulbs and quickly figured that they must have discovered the results of my research in the gym.

Then I was informed that a letter to my father—which would include the bill—was being prepared. That didn't faze me too much, as Papa was way off in America and I figured that by the time he came back the joy of seeing his little treasure again would make him forget the light-bulb incident.

After that they pointed out the potential danger which a

half-darkened school presented and finally they touched upon the moral and ethical aspects of the sordid case and sentenced me to fifteen hours of "Carcer." "To give me time to reflect, repent, and cleanse and purify my soul," as they so nicely put it.

So, the following Sunday, I reported at 6 A.M. to the office of the "Herr Pedell," a sort of glorified superintendent and doorman-watchman rolled into one, and was ushered into the Carcer.

It was a bare room, with only a couch, a chair, and a table. And on that table, waiting for me, was a large assignment of homework, which I was expected to finish during my incarceration and which considerably added to the severity of the punishment.

Around came lunchtime, and when they actually brought me only the traditional prison fare of bread and water, my heart began to sink. So I toyed with the fifteen kronen I still had. (The informer had failed to report the betting, because he himself had been involved.)

I didn't have to toy very long; the *Pedell,* a greedy old slob, grabbed my money and sent out for a large, delicious pot of goulash with *spaetzle,* apple strudel, one liter of wine, which he magnanimously shared with me, and some cigarettes. He also brought me the Sunday papers to read, and a warm glow of contentment settled over the Carcer. I took a nap, and the day passed pleasantly.

Next day in class I explained that I had been too mortified and too crushed by the experience of having been deprived of my freedom to finish my homework. My remorse was greeted with doubt, and I was told that, instead of going home during the next two weekends, I would be given the chance to finish that work in the restful atmosphere of an empty classroom.

But it was not all bad. I loved that school. It gave me a glimpse into a new kind of world.

We had our own riding arena, and, of course, our own horses, and excellent horsemanship was taught. Our instructor, a cavalry officer assigned to our school, started us beginners bareback to develop a good seat, and heavy emphasis was on proper style and elegance. In fact, all our sports were subject to strict etiquette.

We learned to fence, both foil and saber, we had regular military exercises with rifles (which were much too heavy for us eleven-year-olds) and we were taught dancing, always with white gloves and in dress uniform.

We were being trained for a kind of life that was on the way out, that would irrevocably be over five years hence. Nobody, of course, was aware of it then.

When the season ended and we all scattered for our summer vacation, I was really looking forward to the fall term.

In 1910, Papa had bought a small country estate in Egern, on the shore of the Tegernsee, the most beautiful mountain lake in the Bavarian Alps. The two old farmhouses, right on the waterfront, didn't have enough ground to suit Papa's expansiveness, so he started to add acreage. As most of the acreage was meadow, he started to plant trees. But he was an impatient man: young trees wouldn't do. Huge shade trees were purchased from all over the country. There the woodsmen dug wide circles around them, deep down into the earth, until the roots were exposed. When the severe winter came, water was poured over these roots and the soil that still clung to them, and they froze into solid balls. Cranes, pulleys, and tractors lifted them out of the ground, deposited them on huge sleds, and they were ferried across the frozen lake to our property and lowered into their prepared and well-manured holes.

Papa especially loved the smell of pine trees. Whenever he took us children on walks through the woods, he used to say: "Breathe in deeply, children, we are in the woods." (That sentence became a catch phrase in our family whenever something had an especially unpleasant odor.)

So now he wanted to own a pine forest. Four acres were set aside for that project and pine trees arrived by the hundreds. After they had been planted, they were secured with wires to stakes in the ground. For several years it was mostly a forest of wires, and the memory of so many of our guests, when given the grand tour of the place, tripping and falling over those wires, still brings a warm glow of pleasure to my obese cheeks.

Papa also had a passion for fountains and for rock gardens with bubbling springs coming out at the top of them and cascading down. So miles of water pipes were laid—five feet underground, so they wouldn't freeze during the winter.

He also had an inexplicable fondness for pavilions. We had four of them on the property. They were uncomfortable, rustic log cabin types and nobody ever used them, except one at the far end of the garden. That one I put to work to entertain my conquests after I had reached what I thought was the age of maturity.

And right smack in the middle of the "forest" Papa built a pool, not for swimming, but for carp and goldfish. It became my chore to feed them: pot cheese they ate, of all things, and they grew big, fat, and lazy.

But one summer, when we arrived for our vacation, our caretaker, so choked up he could hardly talk, told us that they had all died, each and every one of them. It was a sad tale he recounted; of his anxiety as he nursed them, how his brother-in-law, a veterinarian, had prescribed medicine, so unique, that he had to prepare it himself; how they had poured that priceless concoction into the pool, but all to no avail. There wasn't a single fish left—just the bill for the vet and his medicine, and a broken caretaker's heart.

None of us ever had any deep-rooted affection for fish, so our period of mourning was a short one. But Papa was astonished to find that our two watchdogs were emaciated and that the bill for dog food and the low-grade rice they ate was so much higher during the winter when we were away than during the summer when we were in residence.

That puzzlement was cleared up when the caretaker gave notice and his little girl, a nasty, spindly creature who evidently had not been properly briefed, boasted to us how all winter long they had eaten carp and goldfish, dog food and cheap rice! And that as a result of that thrift they were now able to buy themselves their own little place.

Though Papa was six foot seven tall and protruded like a periscope over every crowd, he insisted on owning a lookout tower. In no time it stood there, thirty-six feet high, proud in its functional ugliness, and in its bowels there were forty-seven steps that led to the top.

Papa went up only once! After that he declared that now that he had seen the view it was no longer necessary to climb those steps. But whenever we had guests, they were practically chased all the way up, usually with me as a guide to point out the breath-taking panorama. Papa sat comfortably at the foot of the tower and supervised the sight-seeing.

Only once, as far as I can remember, was there any practical use for that silly edifice: the Hotel zur Post in Tegernsee had caught fire and we all watched the spectacular holocaust through binoculars.

In our large garden Papa fixed up several shady places. Chairs and tables were placed under trees for outdoor living. We had the Lindenplace, the Mapleplace, the Elm, Beech-tree, and Oakplace.

Whenever the whim to have a *déjeuner sur l'herbe* befell him, the maids had to load up tea wagons with tablecloths, silverware, dishes, and whatever solid and liquid nourishment was to be consumed, and push these two unstable carriages precariously over gravel paths to their designated place.

These meals were always un*gemuetlich* as hell: leaves, insects, and bird droppings fell into our food and there was constant running back and forth, usually by my fleet-footed sister and me, retrieving pills, cigar holders, shawls, or whatever had been forgotten. And everybody, excepting Papa of course, yearned for the comfort of our dining room or the terrace in front of our house, with its proximity to the kitchen.

But the Oakplace was our bête noire. The tree after which it was named was very old and had a huge trunk. And around this trunk some demented carpenter had fashioned a circular bench to which a circular table was firmly attached. These two round pews had two entrances: nimbleness and the ability to slide sideways in a crouching position were required to get in and out. When everybody was seated it was only possible to converse over the left or right shoulder and to crane your neck backward. Whoever was seated at the other side of the tree trunk could not be seen by the other half and could only be heard if he or she were in good voice. Also, everybody was trapped and could leave only after all had gone through the uncomfortable gymnastics of sliding out again.

Papa, who was always the focus of attention, didn't mind, but one day the whole family rebelled, even soft-spoken Mama, and the Oakplace was abandoned.

Just to make sure that it would never be revived, Mama slyly had a beehouse erected very close to it. We never got much honey, but the Oakplace was killed for good.

Papa, who liked to utilize the garden as much as possible, developed the habit of taking his afternoon naps far away from the house, and we had to drag deck-chairs, blankets and pillows, cigars, books, cigar holders, and matches way back to some of our babbling brooks, and after an hour or so drag them back again.

There were two houses on our place—one small and one large. They both had tiny windows, tiny rooms, and very low ceilings. In order to be able to occupy the house in an upright position, Papa raised the ceiling of both floors two feet each. He then enlarged the rooms, breaking out walls, moving staircases and generally changing the structure of the house, which necessitated odd reinforcements and supports, so that we lived with assorted pillars standing in the middle of some of the rooms, most of which were on separate levels anyway. It is still a mystery to me that nobody ever broke a leg.

Of course there was no plumbing, so bathrooms were installed and soon the happy flush of toilets resounded through the house. The local architect, a man of great practicality and good sense, implored my father not to pour so much money into "these two dilapidated antiques," but instead to tear them down and erect a new modern villa. But Papa and Mama, with their highly developed sense of the authentic, had been bitten by the remodeling bug, and after it was all done and finished, they were proven right: We had a jewel of a house, every room immaculate in taste and décor, and all done in the style of the Bavarian countryside.

Papa's study was the smallest room in the house: eight by ten feet, completely paneled in a rare, glossy blond wood and strategically located so that he had a complete view of both the driveway and the main entrance. He was thus in a position to observe and control all goings and comings. He had a positive mania about having to know everything that went on in the house; he had to get the mail first and nonchalantly put aside letters that were not for him—and promptly forgot about them. Of course this played havoc with both my sister's and my youthful romances, so whenever we expected a billet-doux, we waited for the mailman on the corner.

He couldn't stand it if everybody was not home and at his beck and call. Not that he wanted us around him all the time. Far from it. He disliked being disturbed, loved to be alone, but *beware* if Mama went out shopping or my sister or I left the house. He complained loudly that nobody cared for him, and that he was being left all alone all day long. And he wanted to know if these trips were really necessary.

On the very top floor, under the roof, Papa had a photographic darkroom. That was called "Der Katzenlahm." (It means a place so high up that even the cats get lame climbing up there.) There he sat for hours, developing films and printing stereoscopic glass plates of all the pictures he had taken during the winter season. They were catalogued, numbered, listed, and put into trays. These trays were loaded into a large viewer and by pressing a handle were lowered and raised to be observed. He was very meticulous about it, but God forbid if anyone wanted to see the pictures; then he got quite depressed, used many subterfuges, and discouraged it by every means.

I know that there are many thousands of pictures which no one but himself has seen.

In the garden we had a large greenhouse where we grew champignons, flowers, and huge cucumbers. Twice a year, regular as clockwork, most of the windows of the greenhouse were broken by sudden hailstorms. These usually appeared so unexpectedly that nobody had time to lay the protective long pieces of planks over them. There was always great unhappiness, except for the glazier, who called with mock concern after every storm to find out if we needed him.

We had many fruit trees. And I hated them all, because it was usually up to me to harvest them: Gooseberry and currant bushes are a horrid memory. When the time came to put them up in jars, I had my daily prescribed amount to bring in. Most of the jars were never used, because it was uneconomical to transport them from Tegernsee to our winter residence in Vienna, or maybe even to America—besides, they had a habit of exploding after a few weeks. But they still had to be picked: I remember Papa coming down the lane where the bushes stood—seventy-five in each row—watching me critically and admonishing me to pluck the fruit neatly and systematically lest there be waste. And all the time, life was passing me by; somewhere, someone was waiting for me to go swimming or fishing and I complained bitterly about child labor.

Papa usually got up at six in the morning and began the day by singing a few scales. That woke up the rest of the house. Then he went swimming in the lake, which was still steaming, because the morning air was colder than the water. In he plunged, knowing full well that he would never catch cold during the summer, when he didn't have to sing. Only during the opera season did he watch his voice and only then was he troubled by colds.

He swam out a few hundred feet and then called for my mother: "*Gute Liesi, liebe gute Liesi!*" till she appeared, still half asleep, on the balcony and waved to him.

Then he was satisfied!

One day she didn't respond: Papa kept on calling, howling and rolling about in the water like a seal, yelling "*Gute Liesi liebe Liesi*" without knowing that she had gone back to sleep. Suddenly he noticed a man, fully clothed, jumping in the water and swimming toward him.

"Why do you swim with all your clothes on?" Papa called to him pleasantly.

"Aren't you drowning?" he yelled back.

"No, why?"

"Then why the hell do you scream for help?"

"I didn't scream for help, I was calling my wife."

The poor man was furious, and Papa took him to our house, fed him breakfast, and there he sat in one of Papa's outsized bathrobes while I sped on my bike to his house to fetch him dry clothes.

The small house was nicknamed "The Dragon's Den" because it was occupied by my grandmother. The large one, in which my parents and we children lived, was called the "Hunger Manor House," because poor Papa always had to be on a diet; especially during the summer, because it was so hard for him to starve himself while he was working.

His reducing formula had been prescribed by Professor Gaertner, a famous dietician, and the exact amount of every dish he was allowed to have had been stipulated, and it was poor Mama's thankless job to feed a giant appetite with microscopic amounts of nourishment. On our dining-room table in front of Mama's place stood "the enemy." "The enemy" was a deadly accurate scale calibrated down to half an ounce.

First, the scale was carefully balanced; then, the empty plate was put on it and its weight noted. After that, the meat was added—if it was a gram too much, a sliver would be cut off, and if it was short on weight, a few drams would be added. Then, the same procedure continued with the vegetables —on and off—off and on. Mama was very thorough, and, therefore, very slow, and Papa sat there like a hungry lion, waiting and growling for his female to bring him the freshly killed antelope. He glared at the scale—he drummed impatiently on the table. He picked up and laid down his knife and fork and watched his meal being laboriously built up on his plate:

"Oh, for God's sake—half an ounce more won't make any difference."

"Remember what the doctor said—every ounce represents sixty-four calories and—"

"Yes, yes, but hurry up, can't you?"

"Look, *Leo'schi*"—Mama was really unhappy—"I know

how much you like to eat, but if you are too fat, you won't be able to sing the romantic lovers any more—besides, your health—"

"All right, all right, give me the plate . . ." He would grab it. After one minute, the food was gone, and he left the table, muttering how hungry he still was and that he was POSITIVE that goddam scale was all wrong.

Sometimes we had a meal when he wouldn't fight for every morsel of food, but meekly accept what was doled out to him and be agreeable. Mama then loudly praised his will power and character. She never suspected anybody of anything. One day, she walked into his study and saw that our dog, Schnauzi, standing in front of Papa's desk, was holding a rigid point on the middle drawer. When he saw Mama, he barked but kept pointing. Mama opened the drawer and found a two-foot-long Hungarian salami, still in its original tin-foil wrapper.

When Papa was confronted with this edible pontoon, he was deeply wounded. "Now you've spoiled my surprise," he said, a man terribly wronged. "I got that salami for you and the children!" Mama was ashamed of her mistrust and apologized.

For betraying his master, Schnauzi was renamed Judas Iscariot.

Often, around eleven in the morning, Papa would go on a bike ride "for exercise," as he virtuously pointed out. Trust was not one of the traits I have inherited from my wonderful mother. So one day I got on my bike and trailed him to a small inn at the outskirts of our village, where he sat under a shady tree like a contented Buddha and enjoyed a huge *Kalbshaxe* (braised shank of veal) and a liter of foaming beer.

I got so hungry watching that I came out of hiding and joined him.

"Will you tell?" he asked after the first shock of seeing

me had worn off. "Of course not," I replied, "but I also want a *Kalbshaxe*." "My own flesh and blood, blackmailing me," he exclaimed tragically. "It has come to that!"

Only on August 18, his birthday, did he have "*Fressfreiheit.*"

That great day was carefully prepared: weeks ahead he seriously pondered and planned different menus, only to come up with a better idea the next day. And the closer the day approached, the more uncertain he became that he really, but really, had chosen the things he liked best. He liked so many things best it was hard to decide.

August 18 started with a light breakfast, so as not to spoil his appetite. Then came the traditional congratulation ceremony: Papa sat in a large chair that was decorated with flowers. It was before the days of Scotch Tape, when you can stick a flower to anything, so we had to make garlands. Next the staff paid their compliments, and we all brought our presents. Then we children stepped up and said our wish in the form of a poem. Mama wrote them while we were still small; later on we had fun composing them ourselves. The poem was neatly written on a special piece of paper, embellished with flowers and curlicues (in German it is called *Wunschpapier*), then rolled into a scroll, tied with a red ribbon, and ceremoniously handed to him. He followed the poem by reading it while we poor little tykes staggered through the recitation; occasionally he prompted us, but to get stuck was considered a big disgrace. It was always agony, and when it was over, everybody, including Papa, was relieved.

Then the day began in earnest: his first trip was to the Restaurant Bachmayr to eat *Weisswuerste*. It is useless to try to describe to the uninitiated what a *Weisswurst* tastes like; they are light as foam and still have substance. They melt on your tongue, but you still have to chew them ever so gently, and they not only taste good while they are in the mouth, but even on the way down the esophagus they keep haunting you with their flavor. After one has mastered the proper technique of peeling off the skin in two movements, without losing too much time, so the *Weisswurst,* which comes out of piping-hot water, will not cool off, a few dozen of these joyous delights can be put away in no time. Beer should be drunk with them, and a special sweet Bavarian mustard applied sparingly. Papa claimed that mustard ruined their taste, and he ate them with salt. But respectfully I have to differ with him: I think the mustard enhances their wonderfulness.

The *Weisswurst* is to be eaten only in the forenoon. In fact, Bavaria has an unwritten law that no *Weisswurst* should be allowed to hear the midday church bells. If I were quite sure that there will be *Weisswuerschte* in the Great Beyond, the journey across the river Styx would lose much of its fear.

After that little repast, Papa did brisk exercise: he rode on his bike the distance of four hundred yards back to our home.

At lunchtime, the first course usually was crayfish. They were simmered in a sud of dark beer and caraway seed, after an old Czechoslovakian family recipe, and Papa insisted on preparing them himself.

Crayfish should preferably be eaten at home, because it's all but impossible to be dainty about it. Shirt sleeves and an old kitchen towel around the neck are the prescribed costume for it. And it is a time-consuming feast, because every little claw, the tails, the bellies, and the legs have to be thoroughly investigated and sucked out, so that later on there won't be any fearful doubts, gnawing on your conscience, that maybe some tasty morsel was overlooked and left in the shells.

The main course was always a roast, often suckling pig; the head had to be turned away from Papa, because he claimed that all suckling pigs had an accusing look which upset him. Besides, the hind parts *are* better, let's face it.

For dessert, *Marillen* (apricot) *Knoedel,* with the pits of the *Marillen* taken out and replaced by half a lump of sugar. Be sure that it's only half a lump, otherwise, they are too sweet. The dough for the *Knoedel* had to be very light and of equal thickness all around the *Marille.* Slightly browned bread crumbs, powdered sugar, and melted butter were used to crown the dish, and it was consumed in silence. Only contented little sounds were heard, and on and off a grateful look to heaven, with just the white of the eyes showing.

After that, a good brandy, a cigar, and off into the garden for a nap. In the afternoon the local gentry and our friends dropped in, bearing gifts and paying homage to our beloved great man; long tables were set up in the garden to eat the birthday cake and drink coffee. And the big chair with the flower garlands was dragged out of the house and set at the place of honor.

Then came dinner, and often he couldn't eat as much as he had hoped he would: there just wasn't any more room. One day I heard him say a little prayer: "Dear God, please give me a second stomach, I'll give you my belly for it."

Next morning, he didn't dare to step on the scales and sadly went back on his diet.

We had a good-sized garden right on the waterfront, with a sea wall, and a landing place for our boats. Next to it was our bathhouse. As the water was very deep at that particular spot, Papa erected an enclosure with a trap door (which led out into the open lake) so we children wouldn't drown. By the time it was built, both my sister and I swam like fish and the trap door was only for demonstration purposes. We also had a boathouse, with a very large rowboat. Papa was one of the first on the Tegernsee to own an outboard motor. It made a hell of a racket, was not fast (but very heavy), and, to say the least, most unreliable. After ten minutes of driving, it stopped and took two hours to repair. It was an amusing sight when Papa sat in the stern of the boat, next to the motor, all but submerged to the water line, and the bow and half of the boat stuck out of the water.

When he went fishing I was usually taken along in case the motor failed; I was a better mechanic than Papa in spite of his early training as a locksmith, and when the motor conked out completely, I had to row back home. At first I resented being treated like a spare tire, but Papa was a very good fisherman and I learned a lot from him; and as I grew older, these trips brought us very close together. As we sat quietly, with our lines out—I could talk to him about my problems (all in a whisper, so as not to disturb the fish)—and he told of his plans and hopes, his early beginnings, of my grandparents, whom I had not known, and about his youth and his dire poverty.

His father had inherited the family mill in Maehrisch-Schoenberg, in Czechoslovakia, but after many setbacks lost it. He then moved with his wife and only son to Bruenn, where he got a job in a cloth factory. But there was never enough money; Grandmother tried to help out by taking in sewing, and ruined her eyes doing it, and Papa helped out by building bird cages and inkwells with his fret saw.

At fourteen he was forced to quit school and began earning his living. He got a job as a gardener's apprentice, but saw no future in that and learned the blacksmith and locksmith trade. In our house in Larchmont there hang framed his certificate of locksmith apprenticeship and the document he received when he got the title of *Kaiserlich-Koeniglicher Kammersaenger* from Emperor Franz Josef.

When a fellow workman introduced him as a super at the Stadttheater, Papa soon succumbed to the glamour of the theater. His whole life was changed. To stand on that stage, to smell that air—it was all wonderful and unreal.

As he had an excellent ear for music, he soon learned

certain parts the chorus sang, and lustily sang along with them.

One night the famous baritone Adolf Robinson, who had settled in Bruenn after a long and successful international career, made a guest appearance as Tonio in *I Pagliacci*. Papa, who happened to be standing next to him on the stage as a super, protruding out of the crowd, yelled the chorus parts as loud as he could. Robinson turned around, arrested by some quality of the voice he heard. "Report to my dressing room after the opera," he whispered. Papa was scared. He expected a bawling out.

"I think you have a good voice," he told him in his dressing room. "Come to my home tomorrow, and we'll test it."

Papa staggered home in a trance and with his mother began to build the loveliest dream castles for an unbelievably beautiful future.

"Our poverty was suddenly over," he told me, "and in the middle of the night the sun shone brightly for us."

Next day, Robinson confirmed his first impression. He found the voice exceptionally beautiful and suggested that Papa should become his pupil. He predicted that with hard work and the proper study he would have a great future. When he learned of Papa's abject poverty, he offered to teach him gratis. He and his wife became like second parents to him. Mama Robinson, as he called her, taught him to read music and later on spent hours at the piano helping him to learn his songs and opera roles.

Though Papa was interested only in his lessons and lived and thought nothing but music and theater, he still had to keep his job as blacksmith in order to be able to eat. But after a few months, he and his teacher realized that twelve hours of hard work at the open hearth were not compatible with the delicate training of a voice. Late at night, he would arrive for his singing lessons, dead tired and his lungs full of soot and smoke.

Robinson found a way out of this dilemma: he and a personal friend of his, who happened to be the commanding officer of the military garrison in Bruenn, arranged for Papa to enlist in the army (overlooking his extreme youth) and to get a pass three times a week to attend his lessons. And whenever there was entertainment in the officers' mess, Papa had to sing. Thus Papa was able to have over two years of uninterrupted study when an accident forced him to leave the army. He had injured his knee and got a medical discharge.

Then began a hard year for him.

He had grown considerably during his stretch in the service, practically to his full height, and his civilian clothes didn't fit him any more. But he got permission to wear his uniform for a few weeks. At home things had gone from bad to worse. Grandfather had lost his job and had to accept a lesser one. There was hardly enough for him and Grandmother to eat.

So Robinson took up a collection among his well-situated friends. They bought new clothes and got Papa a job as clerk in a lawyer's office. But his interest in the law was nonexistent, and his handwriting was so artistic that it was all but illegible. They soon parted company, and the lawyer, who later became a good friend of ours, often mentioned what a happy day it was for jurisprudence when Papa left the office.

Next he tried to sell insurance—with a hundred-per-cent-negative record. After that he became a salesman for a firm that manufactured plum jam. He had a great sales talk interspersed with little songs. I have reason to believe that he was the originator of the singing commercial; the grocers listened with great amusement, but bought very little. Either his spiel or the plum jam was no good. One day he was so hungry that he ate up all his samples, and that was that.

Robinson then got him an audition with the Stadttheater in Bruenn. He sang the *Pagliacci* aria and was immediately hired. A three-year contract—forty gulden a month the first year, one hundred the second, and three hundred the third. It was more money than he had ever dreamed of being able to earn.

Overnight all need and privation were banished. He could devote all his time to his studies, attend all rehearsals, see every performance from the artist box. He practically lived in the theater—arriving every morning before they opened and being the last to leave. He learned five operas ready to perform during the first year, but he was not considered ready to make his debut.

Then one of the established singers at the opera, the bass Shukovsky, persuaded the general manager to let my father sing Lohengrin at a benefit performance. Papa was up in the part but had never before sung with orchestra, and the rehearsals were a shambles. A catastrophe was predicted. The *Heldentenor* who usually sang the role was standing in the wings in make-up and costume—just in case. But after Papa had sung the phrase *"Elsa, ich liebe dich,"* a sigh went through the house, and the audience applauded and cheered and shouted for over two minutes. The conductor put down his baton and waited. Papa stood there, tears in his eyes, not knowing how to cope with the situation. Never again—though he sang the role of Lohengrin several hundred times—was there applause at that point.

In the second row of the orchestra sat his parents, holding each other's hands and realizing for the first time what kind of glorious life was in store for their boy.

After the performance Papa received an offer to sing in Berlin. The general manager of that celebrated opera house happened to be in Bruenn that evening and caught the performance. It was all a fairy tale come true.

Papa had such a wonderful expressive way of talking. I sat spellbound in the boat, listening, laughing with him, and crying. No wonder I developed a king-sized hero worship for my father.

I have no patience with offspring of famous fathers who turn into bums, drunks, and no-good characters and try to blame it all on the fact that they had to live in the shadow of the famous father. I gladly lived in the shadow that his bright light cast, until I was ready to emerge and make my own way.

After three years in Bruenn, Papa began his engagement at the Royal Opera House in Berlin as Lohengrin.

Young Richard Strauss was the conductor and the famous Emmy Destinn was Elsa. Papa was shaking with nerves and the debut was not too auspicious. One of the reviews the next day read: "A Mr. Slezak from the Civic Theatre in Bruenn sang Lohengrin. He did not wear a beard; he looked like a child and sang like an old man." Papa was crushed. He spent two miserable years there; he didn't get the parts he wanted and was used as a stand-by tenor. Once in a while, generally when everybody else was taken sick, he was given the chance to sing a good role, and then there was always a great show of surprise at the beauty of his voice and his ability: he was reminded of his great youth, urged to be patient, and promised great things for the future.

Finally he got fed up: "I don't have the talent to be a singing civil servant who has to wait for the death of the next in rank," he declared dramatically, and asked for his release. That was an unheard-of thing at a Royal Opera House in the Germany of 1899. He was freed and went to Breslau as first tenor. Breslau then boasted three theaters, one for grand opera, one for drama, and one for operetta. There among the ensemble for the drama was a young actress, Fräulein Elisabeth Wertheim. She was classified as "young sentimental" and had just scored big successes as St. Joan and Juliet. She was considered the rising star of Breslau.

Papa chose *Tannhäuser* for his debut; after the dress rehearsal word spread that the new giant blond tenor had a voice of indescribable beauty and was an excellent actor. The performance was sold out and all the members of the other two theaters who were not working that night milled around backstage to hear the new phenomenon.

During the second act Papa glanced at the people who were standing in the wings.

"I saw a face so lovely, I couldn't believe it! A sudden wave of warmth went through my chest. I stopped singing in the middle of a phrase . . . !" He caught up with the orchestra but all through the act he kept looking at that face, afraid that she might go away before he had a chance to meet her. The moment the curtain fell, he grabbed an assistant conductor, nearly pulling the poor man's arm out of its socket, dragged him to the wings, and commanded: "Introduce me to that lady!" There he implored her not to go away; he would be right back; he just had to take his curtain calls. When he came back, he took both her hands, ignoring the people around him. "My heart stopped beating when I saw you. . . . I will marry you! Please say that you will. . . ."

"Don't talk such nonsense," she laughed. "You are a clown!"

"NO, I am not a clown, I am a most serious man, I swear it."

From that day on, poor Fräulein Wertheim couldn't step out of her home without encountering Papa, who just "happened" to be walking by. He hung around at all her rehearsals, and a steady flow of flowers, letters, and poems flooded her house and her dressing room. Papa laid out a regular campaign to meet her friends so they would invite them together. They all sided with him and arranged "chance meetings." Word of this high-pressure campaign reached the ears of Fräulein Wertheim's formidable mother in Vienna, who took the next train for Breslau. There she ordered Papa to appear in her presence. For that interview, she really put on the dog, speaking in a most cultivated accent and being terribly grand and refined:

"A marriage," she informed Papa, "is out of the question. You may not be aware that I am a descendant of an old aristocratic family, that I have spent a sizable fortune on my daughter's education. She speaks four languages and is a graduate of the Conservatory of Music in Vienna, with a master's degree in piano. She is a LADY."

As sad contrast to such gentility, she mentioned Papa's peasant background, that HIS father had been a common workman, that Papa had not attended school after he was fourteen years old, and that, if it weren't for the lucky fact that nature had given him a very loud voice, he most probably would still be a blacksmith and that she was pained to notice that Papa spoke with a marked Bohemian accent. . . .

At that point, Fräulein Wertheim, who must have been listening in a most unladylike fashion at the door, burst into the room, took Papa's arm, and said simply:

"I will marry you . . . I believe that I love you!" Her appearance and that statement probably saved old Mrs. Wertheim from being either strangled or pushed out of the window.

The same day, Papa announced their engagement in an ad in the papers. But the period of courtship was very trying.

"I have just been informed that your father was a heavy drinker," Mrs. Wertheim would announce. "The engagement is OFF!" After that had been proven a false and malicious lie and a telephone call to my grandfather had been put through imploring him please to stay on the wagon, they were ENGAGED once more. When they went for walks together, very properly arm in arm, and someone dared look at Fräulein

Wertheim, who was not only strikingly beautiful but also well known as an actress, Papa would let go of her arm, stop the ogler, and ask pleasantly if he wanted his nose broken. The six-foot-seven physique of Papa usually brought forth a meek and fast NO. But sometimes that answer did not come fast enough.

Papa won every fight.

As he quite correctly figured that one cannot have two careers and two sets of ambitions running smoothly on the same track and have the kind of married life he was insisting on, Papa decreed that Fräulein Wertheim must quit the stage before they got married.

So Mama obediently said good-by to acting, and I can vouch that she never regretted his decision. Papa was worried that she might not receive enough floral tributes at her farewell performance, so he ordered twenty-five baskets, spreads, and bouquets at different florists all over town, disguised his handwriting and penned little mash notes: "An unknown admirer!" "Never will there be another Juliet like you!" "To the greatest St. Joan of the German stage." "A broken heart sends you anonymous greetings," etc.

February 15, 1900, was a big day for the theater-loving people of Breslau—two of their biggest stars, the operatic idol and the lovely, romantic "young sentimental," stood hand in hand at the altar. The church was packed, and on the sidewalk in a gray drizzle stood the overflow of well-wishers and curious.

But at the very moment the priest spoke the words "I now pronounce you man and wife," the sun broke through like a blessing and a shaft of light shone on the two kneeling figures.

It was a good omen.

4.

THE YEAR WAS 1914. My parents had returned to Tegernsee from their American tour. They had time only to repack their trunks and the following day we saw them off at the station. This time they went to Russia. Papa had accepted a series of guest appearances in Kislowodsk, an elegant and fashionable health resort in the Caucasus Mountains.

Opera festivals were held every summer and most of the members of the Tsar's court vacationed there, trailed by the cream of Moscow and St. Petersburg society.

Artistic standards were very high, all of Russia's best singers and conductors appeared there, including the great and wonderful Feodor Chaliapin, with whom Papa struck up an immediate and lasting friendship.

Papa was fascinated by him, both as an artist and as a person, but he was flabbergasted by the amount of liquor that great man could guzzle—and apparently without ill effect to his voice. It certainly didn't conform with his ideas of what kind of a life a singer should lead. Except during his vacation Papa lived a monastic life. He rarely went out and then only to places where there wasn't too much smoking. He did smoke—cigars—in moderation, but never on the day of a performance.

On such days he had a rigid schedule. He always got up at seven, had breakfast on a tray in his study, and at nine the accompanist arrived. Mama joined them and they went into seclusion in the music room. First vocal warming-up exercises, the study of new roles and new songs, and then reviewing the program for the day's performance.

Mama was his artistic conscience; she knew his voice better than he did himself. She sat in on every study session and all through their lives went to every performance he sang. Papa always knew exactly where in the auditorium Mama was sitting; and after a particularly difficult aria or song, he would unobtrusively shield his eyes against the footlights and look down to her. She would always nod her head in approval, so as not to upset him during a performance, but from the the way she did it, he could tell if it was really good or if she was dissatisfied. She was such a contrast to this glorious extrovert, who one moment would shout for joy and the next be depressed and miserable.

Mama had received an excellent education and had graduated as a pianist from the Vienna Conservatory. She was the most quiet and unassuming person imaginable. So soft, so tender, so gentle. And she never let on that she was a veritable walking encyclopedia, had read everything, knew everything; all one had to do was ask her; her musical instinct and judgment were infallible. She seldom raised her voice and she guided her "Leo'schi," that often childlike, unruly giant with invisible threads of love.

The only arguments they ever had, as far as I can remember, were because Papa ate too much and wouldn't stick to his diet. He would say, "Go ahead, reproach me—when I'll be lying, cold and stiff on my bier, you will be sorry you were so unkind to me." Then Mama would cry and say: "Leo'schi, don't ever say that again, not even as a joke." And Papa kept on eating.

After the study session in the morning Papa kept to himself during the day, so as not to talk and to save his voice. After a light lunch, he took a nap and around four in the afternoon he had tea. But no food until after the opera. He spent the hours before going to the theater in meditation, and deep concentration on his evening's work.

His main thought—always—was to protect, save, and nurse his most precious possession, that mysterious wonderful great intangible—his voice. To be in *good* voice, in top form, to sing correctly, without pressing or undue strain, to be always in full command of his technique—that was his everyday religious chore. That was the basis of his great artistry. Over that he poured his musicianship, his wonderful talent for interpretation, his acting ability—and his great good heart: that undefinable something that spells the difference between an excellent singer and a truly great one.

The rapt attention of his audiences as they sat, completely absorbed and transported, the breathless silence and the almost sacred atmosphere he created in a concert hall, when he sang the songs of Schubert, Hugo Wolf, Brahms, Richard Strauss, and Beethoven—these moments were the best memories of my childhood. I remember one of the great hurts of my childhood when one of my teachers, who had been invited by my parents to one of Papa's concerts, later told my father that he didn't think it was a good idea that I should attend these recitals, because: "The boy beams and gloats as if the applause and adoration for the father were meant for him." I was stunned that anyone could accuse me of such base motives, because I was so proud of him; of course I was also proud to be his son. Later, when I had learned to play the piano well enough to accompany him in his home studies, I took even greater pride in his achievements, because by then I had a better understanding of his work—how every melodic line, every phrase had been polished and gone over and over again, the exact spot where to breathe, the dynamics of the song, everything had been set, nothing left to chance. When Papa sang a song that was new in his repertory, he usually worked from six to eight weeks till he felt he had really mastered it and could interpret it with the authority he always insisted on. He often scorned the easygoing, hurry-up sloppy preparation some young singers employed, who quickly learned the lyrics and the melody and performed the work practically the next day.

The engagement in Kislowodsk was a great success, and the enthusiasm and warmth of the Russian people and especially the fellow singers were most gratifying.

My parents couldn't read the Russian language and there were no German newspapers, so they were unaware that the assassination at Sarajewo had brought Europe to the brink of a world of explosion.

On July 29—at one o'clock in the morning there was a knock at their hotel room; Chaliapin and two fellow singers of the Royal Opera House stood outside:

"Slezak, my friend," Chaliapin said excitedly, "you must leave Russia immediately. War is imminent. You and your wife, as Austrians, will surely be interned and may even be sent to Siberia. We are here to help you."

Papa and Mama got dressed in a hurry and they drove to the theater. They bribed the night watchman to let them in, packed all of Papa's costumes, loaded them on two troikas, and went back to the hotel to get their personal baggage ready.

Chaliapin took care of all the travel arrangements, and they were able to leave Kislowodsk at noon. Most of his Russian colleagues and many members of the orchestra came to see them off. Their compartment was piled high with farewell baskets: enough fruit and cheese, meat and caviar and the inevitable vodka, which Papa—unwisely, I think—never drank—to feed twenty tenors. The train was already filled with military personnel, reporting to their posts, and my parents generously passed out goodies all through the trip.

Only the caviar they ate themselves.

In Moscow the war atmosphere was already at high pitch. Extras announcing the death of Emperor Franz Josef were sold in the streets; Papa, who had always been a staunch monarchist, cried like a child. An hour later it was denied—in fact the old gentleman didn't pass on till the year 1916.

In Moscow they learned that no transportation was possible, all trains had been requisitioned for the army.

But Chaliapin had alerted one of his friends, a high-ranking officer, who was an ardent opera fan. He made it possible for them to leave for St. Petersburg and the Finnish border on the train that carried the Austrian ambassador and his staff. It was the last train out of Russia.

Papa was not permitted to take all of his baggage along, so they carried only a few of his priceless opera costumes and left seven large trunks with personal belongings at a warehouse—with little hope of ever seeing them again. But in 1918, a few months after the war was over, there arrived in Tegernsee the seven trunks; nothing was missing, except that every button had been removed from all garments.

From St. Petersburg they crossed over to Vyborg, then on to Sweden, and headed for home.

We in Tegernsee were naturally terribly worried; we had not heard from them for over two weeks—I had horrible visions of their having been arrested and sent to a salt mine. I was praying and lighting candles. I even made a rash promise to God, that in case He should—please—bring them back safely, I would become a Trappist monk.

Often, when I find myself embroiled in the nasty jungle fights of show business and—unwisely—shoot off my mouth, I think that maybe that hadn't been such a bad idea after all.

I was twelve years old when the war broke out, but I can well remember the lurid headlines about "perfidious Albion," "the archvillain Poincaré," and how peace-loving Kaiser Wilhelm and benign old Emperor Franz Josef, standing shoulder to shoulder, would lead us to glorious victory.

Picture postcards of the two emperors were sold, showing them clasping hands and looking bellicose, flanked by fierce heraldic eagles, holding the German and Austrian flags in their claws.

There was one picture I remember especially well: It was called: "The Emperor in Prayer" and it showed Franz Josef, in full-dress uniform, with white gloves, kneeling on a *prie-dieu,* his eyes transfixed, looking into space. I always wondered how this photo was taken, because I couldn't imagine that the emperor would pose for such a snapshot.

Slogans to create the proper attitude for waging a war were posted everywhere. "God punish England" was one of them, and little humorous poems like:

Jeder Schuss—ein Russ
Jeder Stoss—ein Franzos
Jeder Tritt—ein Britt

Every shot—a Russian
Every shove—a Frenchman
Every kick—a Briton

For me, who had spent most of his years traveling all over the world, it was hard to believe that all our friends in France and England had suddenly become bloodthirsty monsters.

My grandmother hugged me every ten minutes and cried out how happy she was that I was too young to become a soldier.

Then the long-awaited telegram arrived: my parents were safe and two days later we were crushed and smothered by Papa's hugs and caressed by Mama's tenderness.

Everybody expected the war to be over within two months'

time and predicted that "by Christmas our boys will be back home."

Nevertheless, there was talk of possible rationing and "*Gold gab ich fuer Eisen*" (gold gave I for iron) was another slogan which didn't sound too good. It admonished all who owned gold pieces or gold jewelry to contribute them to the war effort. All sorts of methods were used to raise money: In the market place in Tegernsee a wooden monument was erected and for a donation one was permitted to hit a square-headed nail into it. In no time at all the entire wood was covered with nails.

Victory Masses were read and the first of many war bond issues were floated. Everybody was caught up in the waves of patriotism that swept the country.

One evening Papa announced casually that he would be going to Munich the next day. We were a family without secrets, all and everything was always openly talked out, so when he refused to tell us why he would go, we were first baffled and then terribly worried.

We all guessed and speculated until the horrible possibility dawned on us that he might enlist. Mama kept shaking her head and said softly: "No, my Leo'schi wouldn't do such a thing without telling me." But her eyes kept growing bigger and bigger as she said it.

"They wouldn't take him anyway"—Grandmother tried to comfort her—"he's much too fat." All I could think of was: He might lose his voice.

Late at night he returned; I was awake in my bed and rushed out. "Thank God," I thought, "he's not in uniform." I was sent back to bed and Mama and Papa locked themselves into the bedroom. My sister and I listened at the door:

"Leo, how could you? That's terrible!" we heard Mama say with all the reproach her gentleness permitted her.

Papa whispered something about his responsibility to protect his family and his friends—there was more talk which we couldn't understand, except that they were undecided whether or not they should tell the children.

"They'll find out anyway," said Mama sadly.

The next day he spent closeted in his den, refusing to admit anyone but Mama; I got a few peeks in through the door and could see that he was writing down things on slips of paper.

Three days later he sent the gardener and his wife on a short vacation and gave the maids two days off. After everybody was gone, he called us together: "This war, I believe, will last a long time. And the longer a war lasts, the less there is usually to eat. In an hour or so we are getting a few provisions brought in from Munich." He then swore us to secrecy, pointing out that there are people who would consider laying away some staples unpatriotic and call it hoarding!

And that was the reason, he explained, why he had been so closemouthed about his plans and why he had denuded the house of its staff: "—so we won't be at anybody's mercy."

He told me that I, being the smallest, would be the most important on this day. Before I had a chance to ask him why, we heard an automobile horn honking; Papa rushed down to the street and opened the gate. A truck drove up, and Papa locked the gate again.

And then the driver and his helper started to unload the "few provisions"!

200 pounds of coffee, unroasted
300 pounds of sugar
500 pounds of flour
50 pounds of salt
10 pounds of pepper
15 crates full of marmalade
100 pounds of lentils
100 pounds of dried peas

20 pounds of tea
10 pounds of paprika
1000 cakes of soap
100 pounds of chocolate
100 jars of cocoa
200 pounds of rice, and
1000 rolls of toilet paper.

Everything had been put up in five-pound tin boxes and was carried up to the attic. After five hours of hard toil, the truck drivers left, laden with gifts and vastly overtipped.

Papa then produced the mysterious slips of paper. They turned out to be labels and we attached them with paste to every tin can.

Our attic had a double floor. We pried the planks loose and I crept into the narrow crawl space and stowed tin jar after tin jar into the woodwork. It was an exhausting job, but where the roof rose higher, my sister and Mama, and even Papa himself helped. Late at night it was done—we replaced the planks and Papa nailed them down. All the junk that usually fills an attic was pushed back into place and our provisions were well secreted.

Papa had suffered so much hunger and privation in his early youth that he never lost the fear of starvation. He told me that he often had nightmares of becoming impoverished and being unable to provide for his family. He also had another fear: that in his old age he would have to support himself by giving singing lessons. He didn't think that he would have made a good teacher, because to him singing was natural and he believed that what would be good for one pupil might do harm to another. His way of singing was peculiar to the way his throat and his vocal cords were built, and he didn't think he could pass it on.

Fate was kind to him. He never had to starve, and he never had to give lessons.

Two weeks later general rationing was declared, and Papa felt content and wise, that he had been far-seeing enough to provide for his family. And not only for his family, but for all our friends, who were stealthily supplied through the four long years the war lasted.

In 1923 we still had some of the stuff up in the attic, some of the tin cans had rusted through and we were raising a sturdy breed of mice.

And I am positive, that to this day there are still many rolls of toilet paper up there, unless the mice have used them all up.

In 1909, when Papa went to sing at the Metropolitan Opera in New York, we had given up our apartment in Vienna. So for the first few years of the war, we made our base in Tegernsee. It had been decided that I would not return to the Theresianum that fall, because no one of our family would be in Vienna with whom I could spend weekends and Christmas vacation. I was therefore installed in a private boarding school in Munich.

After I had been there six weeks, there broke a beautiful scandal, involving one of the older boys—a strapping lad of seventeen—and the young wife of our elderly *Herr Director*.

That kind lady, so it seemed, enjoyed teaching and educating these eager adolescents far beyond the demands of the regular curriculum. Her husband discovered by chance what kind of homework this student did, and disapproved with great vigor. There was a glorious free-for-all, with a broken nose for Madame and colorful shiners for the other combatants. To preserve my innocence in such a hotbed of lust and depravity, I was yanked out of that morass, enrolled in the Maximilian Gymnasium and placed to board in the pure home of Herr Professor Duell.

Frau Professor was in her late forties, timid, spinsterish, and ill-suited to breaking in future Casanovas.

Herr Professor was stern, severe, upright, and terribly Teutonic.

During the first month of the war, they had lost their only son Helmuth and were eager to have a child in the house. I was given Helmuth's room. A large photograph of Helmuth in uniform hung over the desk. The frame of that photograph was draped with black mourning shroud and pinned to it was the Iron Cross, first class, which Helmuth had received posthumously.

The atmosphere was oppressive: there were Helmuth's bed, Helmuth's desk, Helmuth's chair, Helmuth's wardrobe chest, and all mementos of his young life. He had belonged to a dueling student fraternity; his crossed sabers were attached to the wall and between them hung Helmuth's student cap and his *couleur* ribbon. His books filled the shelves and the desk had not been touched since the day he departed.

"It is a great honor for you," Professor Duell said the first day, "to be allowed to occupy the room of that young hero, who died, sword in hand, defending the *Vaterland*."

It was like living in a shrine. I was afraid to talk above a whisper and to laugh in that room seemed like sacrilege.

Every few days Professor Duell held "inspection"—just to make sure that all was neat in Helmuth's room and nothing disturbed.

Mama was concerned that I might forget the languages I knew so well. She spoke French and English with me whenever we were together. (During the war years we could talk only when we were alone and out of earshot of Germans; to talk the language of the enemy was considered unpatriotic, even treasonable.) She had given me a small book by Alphonse Daudet, *Tartarin de Tarascon,* which I enjoyed very much.

One day, during "inspection," Herr Professor saw the book lying on Helmuth's desk. He erupted into a white fury:

"The French have killed my son," he screamed, "and you dare to bring French books into his room!"

He took the book, tore at it, and threw it into the fire. I was afraid of his towering rage; I cried out that the book had been written long before the war had started. And that I was not being unpatriotic—that I wished I were older and could join in defending the Fatherland.

He looked at me with cold contempt. "You are an Austrian," he said, and left the room.

Papa and Mama were away on a concert tour, so there was no way for me to get in touch with them right away. Papa's lawyer in Munich had carefully investigated Professor Duell's moral background and reputation and had found them beyond reproach. But he was unaware of the atmosphere in his house.

I thought of calling him up and begging to be allowed to live somewhere else, but I was afraid that I would have to enroll in still another school. And I had already made some friends and developed a crush on a girl named Betty whom I had met ice-skating. Frau Professor, a very kind and sensible woman, warmed up to me and made me understand what it meant to lose one's only son and I felt terribly sorry for her and Herr Professor.

After a while, one by one, some of Helmuth's mementos and at last his picture with the black shroud were removed from the room. Only the sabers stayed. But I didn't mind them; in fact they looked quite adventurous.

I continued my music lessons, which were interrupted with the departure of our last guru, who had to enlist. An upright piano was placed in Helmuth's room. I practiced quite a lot and began to compose; naturally I started by writing an opera: I called it *Nero,* and the opening scene had Rome burning and Nero playing the violin. After that climactic beginning I had nowhere to go and the project was abandoned.

Years later I found some of the music and I blush to admit that the fire music was straight out of *Walkuere* and the violin part a complete though unintentional steal from Max Bruch's violin concerto in G minor. And that they didn't fit together.

I also tried to write a requiem for Helmuth, which began with a flute solo that spanned sixty-four bars. My music teacher looked at it and asked: "When does the flutist breathe?"

I was permitted to attend an opera or a concert once a week and saved my allowance till I had enough to invite Betty, my ice-skating romance, to come with me.

Betty was terribly bored with *Goetterdaemmerung* and I was terribly disillusioned with Betty, who incidentally lost all her charm the moment she took off her ice skates.

The highlight of that year remains for me that I was able to commit the perfect crime.

One of our teachers always held Socrates up to us as THE shining example to mold one's life after.

In the Aula, our large auditorium on the second floor of the school, there stood, high in a niche in the wall, a bust of that unattractive, flat-nosed hemlock drinker. We had developed quite a hatred for him and always tried to hit his bust with spitballs.

On Saturday during recreation period in the schoolyard, I stole away and into the Aula.

With the skill of a steer-roping cowboy at a rodeo, I managed to throw the noose of a strong cord around Socrates' head and hung the cord out of a nearby window till it touched the ground outside. Next evening—it was Sunday and the school grounds were deserted—I crept in and found the cord still hanging where I had left it. So my attempt had not been discovered. Making sure that nobody saw me and with my heart beating in my throat, I gave the line a good strong jerk.

The welcome sound of Socrates crashing on the floor and disintegrating into many pieces of plaster of Paris reached my ears and I bolted.

The crime is still unsolved, but my lawyer tells me that I am now protected by the statute of limitations.

In 1916 Papa rejoined his old alma mater, the Vienna Court Opera and I said good-by to Herr and Frau Professor Duell and to Maximilian Gymnasium to begin another adventure in learning at the Piaristen Gymnasium in Vienna.

We rented a beautiful apartment in the very heart of the city; fourteen rooms, on the second floor of the Heinrichshof, a famous Viennese landmark. The view was breath-taking—to the left and right—the wide, handsome tree-lined Ringstrasse and straight ahead the Kaerntnerstrasse with St. Stephen's Cathedral in the background. And opposite us, on the other side of the Ringstrasse, the lovely old opera house.

The location was also most convenient because it eliminated the need for a car. During the war years it was practically impossible to maintain even a horse-drawn carriage, as all the horses had been pressed into the service. And taxis were few and hard to find. So Papa, after having sung a performance, just bundled up, crossed the street and was home.

To judge the exact time of his arrival, all our maids had to do was to look out of the window and see when the opera was over and people started streaming out into the streets. Exactly fourteen minutes later, Papa stomped in and rushed to the dining room, where an elaborate hot meal was waiting for him on the table.

There were two entrances to our apartment, both leading in from the large vestibule up a graceful winding staircase.

One entrance led to Grandmother's suite. But she never used it: she said it made her feel excluded.

She now lived with us permanently. The exact opposite of my quiet, gentle, tender Mama—our O, as we all called her (O was a derivative of *Grossmama, O-mama,* O), could be a holy terror with bursts of temper and fits of rage.

In the tantrum department Papa was no mean slouch himself, and during the first few years of her life tenancy with us there were some memorable encounters.

They always ended with O announcing that she was moving out. The maids had to bring all her bags and trunks up from the basement; but after she was all packed, Papa locked her in her room.

And there she sat on her trunks, all dressed up for departure, screaming and howling. After a while poor Mama, who suffered terribly during these battles, would go in, pacify her, and help her unpack. And after a few hours all was forgotten.

After the war, when inflation in Austria had wiped out everybody who had lived on a fixed income and annuities, O's widow's pension became worthless. But until the day she died she never knew that she was financially dependent on us. Papa had his bank prepare monthly statements for her, showing an income, and when she wanted to buy clothes or presents, he had the bank deliver money to her.

O loved to recall the "splendor of her youth," as she called it. Stories of town houses with major-domos in knee breeches, of hunting lodges, of being presented to the emperor —shining as the most beautiful lady at the court ball, with all the archdukes pushing each other out of the way—just to get a look at her—all these were told again and again and with each retelling we waited impatiently for new embellishments she would add. When the stories became too wild, we expressed doubt, which outraged and made her furious. And then we said: "We will ask Tante Anna if that's true."

Tante Anna, her sister, was her constant nemesis. She would instantly deflate her and set the record straight. O wouldn't even argue, she just said that Tante Anna watched ghosts at night in the cemetery and was touched in the head. Which indeed she was.

From her we learned that she and O had come from a family of second-generation impoverished, very minor aristocrats who were always broke. O had to earn a living, which in the year of 1869 was a very difficult thing to do for a genteel young lady. She took a job as *retoucheuse* at a fashionable photographic atelier. There she met and was successfully wooed by my grandfather, who had come there to pose for his portrait. He was thirty-two years her senior and came from a very wealthy and cultured patrician family. At the age of fifty he had retired from his banking business and now lived as *rentier* on his considerable income.

Judging from what Tante Anna told us, he must have been a saint, the way he put up with this nineteen-year-old, poorly educated spitfire, who was loud, vulgar, and irascible. But he loved her and she became "a good wife" to him. Sadly their first child died, and after that she bore him two boys and two girls. She hated the boys and adored the girls, who were constantly dressed up and primped like dolls.

At the annual flower Corso—a great social event where all and everybody tried to outshine each other—O was riding in Grosspapa's flower-decked open landau, dressed to the hilt, with wasp waist pinched so tight she could hardly breathe. Next to her sat her two lovely daughters, their dresses the same color as hers, wearing large straw hats with ribbons streaming down past their carefully curled long tresses. Each held a delicate basket filled with flowers; these they gracefully tossed out of their equipage to the admiring crowd that lined the street along which the cavalcade moved. They presented a picture of elegant loveliness.

But unexpectedly there emerged from the gawking spectators two dirty little street urchins, in filthy rags. They ran along with her carriage, bleating at the top of their voices: "Mama, Mama, we also want to ride in the parade with you."

O was thunderstruck. At first she tried to ignore them, but the boys, encouraged by the laughter of the crowd, kept up their chorus and even tried to board the landau. Then her fury got the better of her and she lashed out with her umbrella, trying to hit them.

"The day was ruined for me," she wailed, "I was humiliated and made the laughingstock of Vienna."

My grandfather, who had not known about his sons' little joke, nevertheless got hell from her for not having prevented that social catastrophe.

Later on, long after Grosspapa had found peace in eternal sleep, O always spent all our vacations with us, and when my parents were away on short concert tours, where they couldn't take us along, we were in her charge. I don't know if she actually disliked me, as she disliked her sons, but she definitely favored my sister.

When she moved in with us for good, she was sixty-six years old, and the fires had cooled a little. But there was a lot of fight left in the old girl; and the embers of her bad temper still glowed brightly.

After I had grown up and ceased to take her outbursts seriously, I ribbed and teased her quite a lot.

She was immensely curious: she spied on the servants, tried to read their mail, checked what time they came in and stayed up, peering out of the window to find out who brought them to the door. Our gardener in Tegernsee, a rather outspoken diamond in the rough, once said to Papa:

"Hey, *Kammersaenger*, the old grandmother—I don't like

her; during the day she sleeps and at night she snoops." And how right he was. She loved to have other people share secrets with her, which she gave away a minute after she had heard them.

Once, when I was going away on a trip, I handed her a large box which was securely tied and knotted with string.

"O," I said, "please keep that box for me till I return; but you must promise not to tell Papa or Mama about it, in fact I can't even tell *you* what's in it—it's such an important secret."

She looked me straight in the eye, took the box, put it in her closet, and said with confidence-inspiring sincerity: "I promise! I'll hide it in here where nobody will find it, I won't breathe a word about it."

Papa told me later that I had not even gone out of the house when she began to untie the knots; she sweated and cursed because I had drawn them so tight. Inside the box she found another box, just as firmly tied. And a third and a fourth; and the fifth box contained just a note saying:

"Hello, nosy, you broke your promise!"

Her screams could be heard a mile away.

One day I told her that somebody had given me a hot financial tip for her: she should buy balloon stocks; they were sure to rise. Papa was not home, so *she* called the bank and asked them to get some of the stock for her. After a hilarious conversation, which I overheard on an extension, she found out that it was a joke. She threw a chair at me.

She lived to be ninety-six years old and was always strong and healthy as a moose, but if someone asked her how she felt, he got a long list of complaints. Doctors who found nothing wrong with her were branded as idiots and quacks, and when I told her how well she looked, she erupted: "Don't anger me—I am sick."

After she had turned eighty-five she hardly left the house any more; she just sat at the window, looking down at the

Ringstrasse, and all that really interested her was what kind of business the shoeshine man, who had his stand across the street at the corner of the old Bristol Hotel, did every day. She counted his customers and pitied him when it rained and he was not at his stand.

When we moved to Tegernsee in the summer, she complained: "It's dull—everything is green." And she wanted to go back to Vienna and her window seat.

During her last few years she all but lost her memory: though my mother died in 1944, and O lived in the same house with us, Papa managed to keep this sad news from her. She would ask ten times a day: "Where is my Elsa, why doesn't she come to see me?" And Papa said: "But *Mutterl*, she was just here, just two minutes ago, and you had a long talk."

"Oh yes, so she was," she would reply. "I guess I am getting forgetful." And she was satisfied.

5.

THE LOEWENBURGISCHE CONVICT in the Piaristengasse in Vienna became my permanent home for the next four years. It was managed by the Piarists, a Catholic educational order founded by Joseph of Calasanza in Rome at the beginning of the seventeenth century. The Piarists taught chiefly in Italy, Spain, Germany, and in Austria. Their reputation as educators rivals that of the Jesuits.

Our school was spacious and comfortable, in a building that was erected around 1760. It was a strictly parochial school with rigid discipline.

But alas, it was not as fancy or elegant as the Theresianum; and that's why my parents enrolled me there. They sensed a change in the air and felt that it was no longer the time to raise Little Lord Fauntleroys.

We had to wear uniforms, comfortable fatigues in school, but when we went out it had to be gala dress: high dark blue cap with silver cockade, dark blue double-breasted tunic with silver buttons and stiff high collar, long pants with narrow stripe, long military coat with epaulettes, sword, and white gloves. In cut and silhouette it was very similar to the Austrian officers' uniforms.

The food was terrible: starchy, monotonous, and barely enough to fill our growing young stomachs. And during the winter we had practically no heat. All was blamed on the war, but some of the older boys who had been there several years insisted that it had been just as bad during peacetime.

The dormitories were especially cold. My room, which I

shared with three other boys, was known as "Little Arctic"; I slept with four blankets and a hood over my head. The moment I dreaded most was when the morning bell clanked —loud, brutal, and merciless—and I had to get out of my warm bed and step into the subzero temperature of our room to get dressed. So I learned—and soon became quite adept—in putting on all my clothes, including socks and shoes, pants and tunic, in a prone position, while staying in bed under the warm blankets.

This technique came in very handy later in life, when I had to travel in upper and lower berths on trains and planes.

Only once was I unable to use it. About eight years ago I had to fly from New York to California and the only space I could get on the sleeper plane was an upper berth. The airline manager kindly let me board the plane before the other passengers came on and I viewed this upper with its low ceiling with great misgivings; but I bravely undressed in the aisle—climbed up the ladder and with the help of the copilot wedged myself sideways into that low and narrow sepulcher.

The stewardess helpfully hung my clothes on a hanger at the foot of the bunk, together with my shoes. She showed me how to fasten my seat belt, warned me not to smoke during take-off, wished me a good night, and closed the curtains.

During the night I had to pay a visit to the little boy's room, but to my growing agony I discovered that I was unable to reach my clothes at the foot end of the bed because I couldn't sit up. If I raised my head more than eight inches, I banged it against the ceiling, and my round firm belly, protruding upward, all but kissed the roof of my six-foot bungalow.

With my toes I tried to get a grip on the coat hanger, but evolution had denied me the dexterity it had lavished on every silly chimpanzee.

I rang for the stewardess, whose offer to help I had to decline, because I wore a pajama top, and asked for the copilot. The copilot, she informed me after about twenty minutes, was busy because we were flying into some turbulence, and she told me to fasten my seat belt.

Help finally arrived: the navigator crawled up the ladder, slipped pants on me, and pulled me out of my receiving vault. I sat up the rest of the trip!

Our school chapel received us every morning for Mass. I became an altar boy: partly out of true devotion, and partly—I suspect—because I enjoyed wearing cassock and surplice, pivoting with the heavy Mass book when I carried it around, and genuflecting and swinging the censer with great vigor.

I usually assisted at Mass for Father Lodovico, who, because of his fondness for wine, was nicknamed Father Lush.

During the ablution the altar boy pours water and wine out of two small cruets over the thumb and forefinger of the priest; when I poured the wine, which I always did with my right hand, Father Lush held the chalice motionless. But when my left hand, which held the cruet with the water started pouring, he quickly stopped the flow after a few drops, by slightly raising and gracefully turning the chalice away.

One morning the Mr. Hyde in me got the better of the Dr. Jekyll; I switched cruets.

Crystal-clear water poured from the little carafe on my right and just a few teardrops of wine were permitted in the goblet.

Father Lush began to drink: his eyes, which were always half-closed during ablution, opened slowly—in disbelief! He turned toward me! My little angel face was bathed in innocence. He kept staring at me as if to discover the motive for this unkind deed.

After Mass, in the vestry, he didn't speak to me, but as he left he said darkly:

"Boy, don't *ever* do that again!"

The next morning—I swear I didn't do it on purpose, it was an accident, I was probably nervous—the cruets were switched again.

That day my career as an altar boy ended and Father Lush was my true friend no longer.

Our father rector, who had the disturbing habit of tapping the school desk with his pencil to attract our attention and was therefore named Father Tap Tap, liked to utilize whatever talents his pupils possessed for the good of the school. He of course knew of my interest in music. Besides taking piano lessons, I studied harmony, counterpoint, and composition. Lessons on the organ were added; I got great enjoyment out of it, especially as I was allowed to practice on the big organ in the beautiful old Piaristen Kirche, next door.

In our chapel we had just a simple instrument, two manuals, ten registers, and twelve-foot pedals. After a while I was considered good enough to play at Mass.

Paraphrasing between the regular hymns became my favorite activity. It stimulated my creative urges. A popular song of that time was called "Babydoll, You Are the Apple of My Eye"! It had a fast beat, sort of a marching rhythm, and I used its theme in many variations, as obbligato and in little snatches of a fugue, because I had discovered that by playing it slowly and in a minor key, it could be made to sound very much like a hymn.

Father Lush, who was the worldliest of our priests and had probably been exposed to that minor masterwork outside the convent, recognized it. All hell broke loose!

I was accused of irreverence, blasphemy, sacrilege, and

all-around wickedness. And the privilege of playing the organ at Mass was withdrawn.

I was terribly hurt because it had not been my intention to offend, but I put on a bold "I don't care" front and even bragged that I had done it on purpose, so they would fire me and I could sleep a little longer in the morning. (Altar boys and organists had to get up earliest.)

Father Lush of course heard about my boasts and I was promptly ordered to report for *"Orgel melken."*

"Milking the organ"—that's what we called the laborious procedure of pulling the two ropes that were attached to the bellows and thus provided a steady flow of air for the organ pipes.

I was furious and humiliated to have been downgraded to such manual labor, especially as I considered my replacement as organist vastly inferior to me.

I brooded revenge, and soon discovered that the organ would function properly only if the milking was done in a steady rhythm. So I began missing every fourth or fifth stroke, which resulted in the air giving out. The music wheezed out like a deflated balloon, only to come up again to pitch when I restored the influx of air.

I was really disgraceful. And this time I was severely punished: my weekends at home and my opera privileges were canceled for three weeks.

So that my musical education would not be neglected Papa had made arrangements for me to attend one opera or concert a week. He also got me a pass to the standing-room section of the Hofopernhaus.

Standing room was patronized by the rabid, ardent opera buffs and music lovers who didn't have enough money to buy seats. For many many hours before a performance, sometimes half through the preceding night, these valiant and knowing enthusiasts stood in line, braving rain and snow, wind and ice

—to be able to buy one of the limited quantity of admission tickets and to occupy the various choice locations.

The most desirable spots were the narrow spaces in the left- and right-hand corners of the orchestra standing room, front row—at the railing.

They were called the "*Kipferln*" (that's Viennese for horn-shaped rolls).

In one of the *Kipferln* you could rest your front against the railing, your back against the wall and wedge one side of your anatomy between wall and railing. You were thus supported on three sides and the load on your feet was a light one.

And nobody could block your view. The railing also made a handy support for the piano score, which many, including myself, used—flashlight in hand—to follow the opera.

At 7 P.M. the gates were opened and spilled this hardy and persistent group into the auditorium. They raced each other up the stairs and arrived, exhausted and out of breath, in the standing-room section. You can imagine their fury when they found that one of the two *Kipferln* was already occupied. Occupied by me, who had come in through the stage door and stood there, trying to look aloof and unconcerned—but dripping with bad conscience and very much afraid.

The first time it happened they started to throw me out, but one of them called: "Ah, let him go—it's the Slezak kid."

As they were all fans of Papa they let me stay, but that evening I left with a long list containing the names and addresses of all those who wanted to have personally autographed pictures of Papa. And I was warned that I had better deliver—or no more *Kipferln.*

My most treasured musical memories, which I wouldn't trade for anything in the world, stem from this time. True, I had heard much wonderful music, and many many evenings in Vienna, New York, and Paris stand out. But Papa had taken me by the hand and guided me to their beauties. Now I was old enough—and had learned enough to hear for myself.

The librarian of the opera was kind enough to lend me whatever scores I wanted, including those of new works. And—for the first time—I heard *Elektra, Der Rosenkavalier, Ariadne auf Naxos, Die Frau ohne Schatten, Die aegyptische Helena, Intermezzo, Salome, Feuersnot, Josephslegende*—and all with Richard Strauss conducting his own works.

During Christmas and Easter vacations I hung around all orchestra and dress rehearsals and had a chance to observe and admire that genius—doubtless the greatest composer since Richard Wagner. Strauss was also one of the best and most sensitive Mozart conductors of his time, and to watch him work with the orchestra, always quiet and in full authority, was a true joy.

In 1919 he became director of the opera. In order to tie him permanently to Vienna, the city gave him the Belvedere Schloess'l, a small château, on a ninety-nine-year lease. And Strauss gave the city the original orchestra score of one of his greatest operas, *Der Rosenkavalier,* which can be seen today at the Oesterreichische National Bibliothek.

He and Papa were very fond of each other and gave many recitals together. The only complaint that Papa had, when Strauss was accompanying him on the piano in some of his songs, was that Strauss always hurried the tempi. Papa wanted it slower, and Strauss said:

"Ah, go on—it isn't *that* beautiful."

Shortly after the war they had contracted for a series of recitals in Holland. (Dutch guilders were a solid currency, not like the Austrian kronen, ravaged by inflation.)

Two days before their departure they each received a telegram from the state department in Berlin, advising them that the man who had arranged these concerts was a much-wanted criminal and suggesting that they cancel the trip. Strauss wired back: "If I chose to do business only with people who are not criminals, I would have to give up my profession."

He could be very witty—but always in an easygoing, *gemuetlich* sort of way: When told that it had taken Hans Pfitzner seven years to finish his opera *Palestrina,* he said: "Well, why does he compose, if he finds it so difficult?"

When Erich Wolfgang Korngold, at the age of fifteen, wrote his opera *Violantha* and in his youthful zest overorchestrated a bit, Strauss said: "You see, one shouldn't give a celesta to a child!"

An ultramodern piece of music was offered at a concert in Vienna. Asked what he thought about it, Strauss replied that he couldn't understand it. "But this is DA DA-istic music," he was told. "Oh," said Strauss with a straight face. "In that case it's hard to judge it at the first hearing. I would have to hear it DAda-CAca-POpo!"

A hefty prima donna was named by him "The Prima-Ton." He was an excellent businessman and very money-conscious. Matters pertaining to income and expenditures were of great concern to him.

In my collections of musical manuscripts, I have thirty-two letters written by Strauss, which were left to me by my uncle, a well-known lawyer in Vienna, who represented Strauss and doubled as one of his partners in the game of skat. One of these letters deals exclusively with garbage removal. Strauss felt that the gift of his little château by the city of Vienna should include gratis removal of trash and the city of Vienna felt that it shouldn't. Needless to say, Strauss won.

Papa would often call him and ask if I could attend some special events at his box. The loge of the Herr Doctor, as he was called, was always packed and I was lucky if I could stand in the back. But thus I was able to see the premières of *Ariadne* and *Frau ohne Schatten,* both with Maria Jeritza and Lotte Lehmann, and the revival of Strauss's seldom performed early work *Die Feuersnot,* Pfitzner's *Palestrina,* the Puccini *Tryptich: Il Tabarro, Suor Angelica,* and *Gianni Schicchi*—and many others.

Pauline Strauss, the energetic and outspoken wife of the great Richard, presided over the box. She ruled him with an iron hand and often complained that, when young, she had had the chance to marry an officer and instead she got stuck with "that musician." She had been a third-rate singer when Strauss was a very young conductor, and she sang a role in one of his first works. During a stage rehearsal Strauss criticized some musical transgression she committed; she thereupon took the score, hurled it at him in the orchestra pit, and yelled:

"Why don't you sing that trash yourself!" and walked off the stage. Strauss proposed the same evening.

Pauline had a loud voice and her comments during a performance, her caustic remarks about everybody, including her husband as a composer, could be heard halfway through the house. She had an uncanny knack of always picking a moment when the music was pianissimo to let go with a good verbal barb.

It was always hard for me to go back to school after leaving the opera, with the thought that after that world of glorious music and enchantment and fantasy I would have to study Latin and Greek the next morning.

All teachers in our school were priests, with the exception of our history teacher, Professor S.

He was short, heavy-set, and always wore formal cutaway, with old-fashioned plastron and vest, high collar, so tight that it cut into his heavy jowls and created overlaps of flesh under his chins.

He was very proud of his square-cut beard, which lent him great dignity; his bushy eyebrows were separated by a bulbous nose with long hair sticking out of the nostrils. He had small beady eyes which were grotesquely enlarged by half-inch-thick lenses in his gold-rimmed glasses.

Every Sunday he appeared at Mass with his whole family. They always arrived in formation, like an Alaskan dog-sled team: the smallest two kids in the lead, behind them two bigger ones, third, two still bigger ones, and the next pair was mother and daughter, both unattractive. And behind them came Herr Professor, walking with his jerky limp, one of his legs was shorter than the other. We expected him to crack a whip and yell: "Mush, mush!"

His history lessons were always highlighted by little comments intended to demonstrate how morally corrupt certain Latin nations were and how upright and virtuous, how ethically and piously the Germanic people had always conducted themselves.

He was against levity, against lust, against sin—and all for the sanctity of the home and connubial purity.

We admired him very much, but we didn't like him.

At the age of fifteen I was already quite tall and on my walks back to school after attending an opera I was sometimes accosted by nocturnal maidens of joy, who were attracted by the uniform I wore. But when they got a good look at my face and saw that I was a schoolboy and not a potential customer, they quickly walked away.

After all, time is money.

I enjoyed these encounters very much—they made me feel grown-up and wicked.

One night I noticed a couple coming out of one of the little hotels which were hidden away in the dark side streets and were patronized by these erring sisters.

The two waved a casual good-by to each other and walked away—each in another direction.

There was something about the man which aroused my incredulous curiosity: he was short, heavy-set, and walked with a jerky limp that I knew so well. I couldn't believe it—it couldn't be true—that champion of marital fidelity wouldn't do that! But I wanted to make sure—so I fell into step with him and at the next street light I was able to execute a snappy salute:

"Good evening, Herr Professor S.!"

He swung around—thunderstruck: "What are you doing here?" he hissed, with all the color having gone out of his red face.

"I am on my way back to school," I replied. "I had permission to go to the opera!"

He lived near our school, so we walked back together—in complete silence. I felt sorry for him, but I also felt like laughing, because he had always been so pompous and such a pillar of virtue.

I was smart enough not to mention the incident to anyone in school, because I knew that such an accusation, supported only by me as a witness, might not be believed and that I could be expelled for maligning a member of the teaching profession.

Professor S. never called on me in class again—he didn't flunk me, but ignored me completely; and that neglect, it comforts me to believe, is the reason why—up to this day—I am completely ignorant of what happened during the Crusades, know nothing about the vicissitudes of the Ottoman Empire, and even less about the War of the Roses.

Every year Papa sang at a church concert for our school. I am sure that I would have been able to graduate without that friendly gesture, but it sure created a benevolent atmosphere for the final exams.

Incidentally, Father Lush not only forgave me, but became my sponsor at my confirmation and on special occasions I was allowed back on the organ—as performer, not as milker!

I wanted to become a composer and conductor; Papa talked me out of it.

Whenever I brought him a new composition, he would listen to it with great interest and then point out where I had lifted that melody or this passage. Since my earliest childhood I had retained in my memory so much music that I was not aware that what I wrote was not original. But after a while I had to admit myself that the genius to create great music was not one of the gifts the muses had laid in my cradle.

With the notable exception of Arthur Nickisch, Hans von Buelow, and a few others, the conductors at that time who were "stars" were mainly great composers, like Strauss, Gustav Mahler, and to a lesser degree Felix von Weingartner. The heyday of a Toscanini, Stokowsky, Furtwaengler, Bruno Walter, Reiner, Leinsdorf, Koussevitzky, Mitropoulos, Beecham, Von Karajan, and all the other prima donnas of the baton had not yet arrived.

Papa readily admitted that I would make a talented musician, but he must have had well-founded doubts that I had in me the stuff to become great. He didn't want me to wind up as a musical employee at some opera house.

But if the searing flame of dedication and calling had truly been blazing inside of me, it would have singed all resistance and advice.

I am afraid I was just a sparkler.

6. Two THINGS PREVENTED ME from becoming a doctor of medicine.

1. The sight of blood made me sick;

2. I saw an ad in a newspaper: Dr. Krakauer back from vacation.

I happened to know Dr. Krakauer. He was fifty-two years old, a well-respected physician, and had practiced his trade for twenty-four years. Reading that ad set off a whole chain reaction of thought.

What kind of life was I letting myself in for?

The study of medicine takes six years; after that I would have to put in around three to four years of postgraduate work and internship at a hospital. I then would have to borrow the money to equip an office and hang out my shingle. After twenty years, after having built up a good practice, always chained to the same city, the same place—I would have to insert an ad in a newspaper to let my patients know that I was back from a couple of weeks' vacation.

Was that the kind of life I wanted?

My childhood was spent in travel. We were always on the move; and suddenly the thought of having to spend the rest of my life in one spot brought on an attack of oppressive claustrophobia: a fear that the humdrum of bourgeois life would make me miss what was going on in the rest of the world.

I wanted to run, run away while it was not yet too late, and that is exactly what I did. I hung up my rubber gloves, turned in my forceps and scalpel, sold my medical books, and confronted my parents with the sad fact that in future they would not be treated for free by their son, the doctor, but, when sick, would have to shell out good money like everybody else.

But what profession to choose? Composer and conductor had been eliminated. I had a great desire to be an opera singer like Papa, but as I had no voice, it had to remain a desire. I came up with an idea: I would become a banker: high finance, the building of a great fortune, controlling whole industries, dictating the rise and fall of the stock market—that was my vision. To close deals in far-off places, investigate mines and oil fields, one has to travel. It sounded like an exciting life. Furthermore—and that thought may have been decisive—I didn't know any poor bankers.

In order to learn the business from scratch, to receive the best all-around schooling, a small bank where I might come into contact with all phases of banking was advised. The banking house of Lewis & Selig was given the honor of receiving me, and for some miraculous reason they agreed to take me on as office boy apprentice.

At first my job started at 7:30 A.M. I had to wait in front of the closed office until the trusted employee with the keys arrived and opened up. Once inside, I hurriedly put sawdust on the floor of the large "Clients' Waiting Room," sprinkled it with water, and swept it clean. I then filled all the inkwells, emptied the ash trays, sharpened the pencils, and tidied the desk of the boss. For the rest of the day I was in charge of the copybook. Every letter written or received, every sales slip on all transactions, was moistened with a special solution and then pressed onto the pages of the copybook. The typewriter, mind you, had long since been invented and, with it, the idea of using carbon paper. But at Lewis & Selig nearly everything was still written in longhand, presumably to give me employment.

Around lunchtime I turned into a fleet-footed messenger, running to and from a little kosher restaurant, bringing nourishment to the clerks who had to stay during the lunch hour and take care of the shop. Our boss, of course, went home for lunch and a little siesta, as was then and still is today the most sensible custom in Vienna.

Most of our clients were Orthodox Polish Jews, with long beards and *payes*—long, curled sideburns dressed in the traditional kaftan, always carrying an umbrella and always wearing a round black hat, which they never removed.

From 10 A.M. to 3 P.M., the time the stock market was in session, they filled the waiting room. All played the market. Every order for selling or buying was relayed by telephone to our customer's man at the exchange, executed, and reconfirmed by phone. The ticker tape on the stock board, that wonderful device that instantly records every transaction for everybody to see, was not then invented. After a while, I noticed that the figures that were telephoned from the exchange were seldom correctly repeated to the clients; there was always a small margin of profit for the bank in every quote. I caught on pretty quickly and sometimes, when business was very brisk, I was assigned to a phone; my larcenous soul flourished like a tropical garden.

One day the phone went on the blink. In dire emergency I was told to try to get on the exchange floor with a large selling order. Only accredited members with a pass were allowed, so I had to crash. I did this by walking up to a stranger who was on his way in and telling him an outrageously dirty story, which made him howl with laughter. The guard just looked at the laughing man, overlooked me—and in I was.

I made my way to the location on the floor that had been described to me, and watched our customer's man working. I heard that the stock that was supposed to be sold was several points above the selling price specified in my order, and got so fascinated watching it being bid up, that I didn't turn in the order until it had risen about twelve points. It was then sold at what turned out to be the peak of the rise. The bank made a good profit, the client just got the price he had specified in his order, and I was only mildly reprimanded.

A few weeks later, I received a pass to the exchange and so became their youngest customer's man. Youth, as far I can remember, was my only distinction.

One day the boss called me in. He told me to close the door, assumed a fatherly air, informed me that he had been watching me for some time and had detected in me an especially fine sense for business . . . "*seachel,*" he called it. He then entrusted me with a very responsible transaction: he handed me a one-thousand-lira bank note, told me that it was a forgery which somebody had palmed off on him, and asked me to go downstairs to the Café Adler and get rid of it.

The Café Adler was called "Die Nachboerse," meaning a place where deals were made after 3 P.M., the time when the regular stock exchange closed. There they also dealt in foreign currency, and one could buy everything except a cup of coffee.

I entered nonchalantly, asked the head waiter at which table lire were handled, sat down, and waited. After a while, a sinister-looking man sat next to me and asked me what I had. "A thousand-lira note," I replied. "I want it changed into small bills."

"That's fifteen per cent handling charge," he said, took my bill and pocketed it without even looking at it (which to this day still puzzles me), and handed me eight hundred fifty lire.

At the office we found that, of the eight hundred fifty, two hundred were phonies—the rest, however, were genuine. I was told that I showed promise and was likely to succeed.

At the exchange I met General Director Mueller of the Internationale Handelsbank. He was a fan of Papa's and took a fatherly interest in me. He thought that I was wasting my time at Lewis & Selig and invited me to come over to his bank, where I could really learn the business.

There I was introduced into the mysteries of double-entry bookkeeping. It bored me to death.

The only glorious compensation was a very attractive secretary, who managed to keep my interest in banking alive. During and after office hours.

Whenever a yearning for feminine companionship became so strong in me that it threatened to impair my efficiency as a bank clerk, I signaled to the object of my affection an SOS of passion and took out of my desk—sly, devilish fiend that I was—a cardboard sign on which was printed the authoritative legend: "OUT OF ORDER."

I then repaired to our trysting place. It was a telephone booth, fairly large as telephone booths go and inside heavily padded and soundproofed. And it had only one tiny little window!

I hung the "OUT OF ORDER" sign outside on the doorknob, unscrewed the electric bulb inside, and waited. After a short while my paramour slipped in and there we were, in pleasant darkness, snug and comfortable in our enforced proximity, sharing that special brand of happiness that goes hand in hand with the nibbling of forbidden fruit.

The only small drawback to our idyllic *buen retiro* was that the booth always smelled of stale cigars. And up to this day that smell recalls pleasant memories.

It is a great tribute to the power of the printed word that nobody ever questioned the message on our sign outside the door and that no eager busybody felt moved to call in a repairman.

After a few months, rumors of my amorous activity and a

general laxity in morals reached the ears of General Director Mueller. He called me into his office and allowed that I might be laboring under a misapprehension as to the purpose of his bank. He insisted that the personal happiness and well-rounded sex life of his secretaries and apprentice bookkeepers were not the sole driving motive for him to stay in business and that I —God dammit to hell—better streamline my activities more along the lines of general banking; that he was transferring me to a department where temptation would not be winking at me from every padded telephone booth, because the youngest female in that department was sixty-two years old and unattractive at that.

He ended his speech, quivering with well-controlled indignation, by announcing that he was not running a brothel, but a bank. A superfluous statement if ever I heard one.

My new exile was the arbitrage department. In the early twenties, inflation was rampant in Europe and arbitrage managed to cash in on that horrible state of affairs.

Let me explain: After 3 P.M., the time the exchange closed, telephone connections were made with, let's say, Zurich and Paris. You ask Paris: What is your bid on dollars?—and you ask Zurich: What do you ask for dollars? If there was a margin of profit, and there nearly always was, the deal to buy and sell was closed on the phone.

It was necessary to speak languages fluently, and while one man talked on the phone, another had to do some quick figuring: For that we used a long, sausagelike device called the "Loga."

I was pretty fast with figures, so I became one of the Loga assistants until they found out that I spoke French. One day they hung a phone on me and that became my job. Of course I was not authorized to deal independently, but it sure was better than bookkeeping.

I got a lot of enjoyment out of the excitement of those

often-shouted telephone deals, and the money I made was more than I had previously earned in bookkeeping, as we received a small cut of the profits.

After four months, based on sheer gall and hints about my indispensability, I even managed to get a raise. My office hours were also changed: because we worked late in the afternoon, sometimes till midnight, I didn't have to come to the office until 2 P.M. Leaving late at night, I felt morally justified in making the rounds of the more fashionable night clubs and bars; and thus the course of my life was changed again.

One night, around 11:30 P.M., I strolled into the Sacher Bar at the Opernring, sat down, and ordered a scotch and soda (not because I liked scotch, but because that drink was considered fashionable). I smoked a long cigar and assumed the bored, blasé attitude befitting a roué and man of the world. A few tables away were seated two men and a woman. The woman pointed at me—the two men turned around and looked me over carefully. I recognized her—she was Lucy Doraine, then a famous motion-picture star. She smiled at me—I smiled back—rather discreetly, so as not to arouse jealousy in her companion. (You see, I was a man of the world.) Then one of the two men got up and walked over to my table, sat down and said:

"With your kind permission, I have imagined you."

That sentence was delivered with a straight face and the thickest possible Hungarian accent. I must have looked very stupid, because he continued:

"You do not understand—you are my vision."

For a moment, I thought an escaped lunatic was talking to me and I was ready to humor him.

"Of course, I understand."

"No, you do not," he said sadly. "But I will explain. My name is Michael Kertesz. I am preparing *Sodom and Gomorrah*, the legend of sin, and we need beautiful young man—and you are beautiful young man."

Slowly the nickel dropped. I remembered the name—he was a well-known film director and the husband of Lucy Doraine. . . . He was probably talking about a film.

I was flattered to be called a beautiful young man, so I took my scotch and soda and joined their table. The other gentleman's name was Ladislaus Vajda, a well-known writer and the author of that forthcoming supercolossal production *Sodom and Gomorrah.*

Kertesz asked me what business I was in.

"I am a banker," I replied with quiet dignity.

"That's not good," said Kertesz. "We want an actor—but who knows, maybe you have talent."

They told me the story of the film. The prospect of playing love scenes with Lucy Doraine was quite tempting.

Two days later, at 9 A.M. I found myself at the Sascha Film Studio in Sievering. A make-up man set to work on me: charcoal black lines around my eyes, penciled eyebrows, red lips—a complete stranger, looking like a store mannequin, stared back at me from the mirror.

I was then led in front of a camera that was cranked by hand. Open arc lights were pointed at me until I was almost blinded. I then took my "acting test."

I had to walk toward the camera to a certain spot, turn to the left to show my right profile, to the right to show my left profile, look up—look down, smile, look sad, wistful, surprised, angry; pantomime "I love you," sit down, light a cigarette, get up again, and walk out.

That was all. They removed the make-up, in the process of which they managed to smear most of the charcoal into my eyes, and I was sent home—blinking and red-eyed like a rabbit.

The next day I was told that I had passed the test and should go and see the producer, Mr. Arnold Pressburger.

As I sat in the waiting room with several other people, they called Mr. Slezak. Before I had a chance to rise, another man got up and was ushered into the producer's presence. I was quite surprised, because Slezak is not a common name in Vienna. Later, however, I found out, that that was a ruse of Mr. Pressburger: He wanted to demonstrate to me that there was nothing special about the name Slezak, just in case I should try to cash in on my father's fame.

He offered me a contract with fourteen times as much money as I made in the bank, but there was a hitch: I was underage and Papa had to countersign that contract.

I knew that he would be less than enthusiastic about my giving up a solid occupation like banking to become a moving-picture actor. At that time film stars did not command the impressive social standing that today is awarded to the stalwarts of our profession. Papa was in Karlsbad, a resort town in Czechoslovakia, for a series of concerts. And by a lucky coincidence, Herr Director Mueller was also there, taking the baths. Rather than write or phone, I took the next train.

When Papa learned of my desire to become a movie star, he behaved like King Lear on the moor:

"'How sharper than a serpent's tooth it is to have a thankless child!'" he wailed, storming and raging against a fate that had afflicted him with such a misbegotten offspring. Then he slapped my face and ordered me to return to Vienna and my job at the bank.

I was only nineteen. Two more years until I came of age, I knew that nobody would hire me without my father's consent, so I pretended to accept defeat.

But early the next morning, before boarding my train, I called on Herr Director Mueller. I told him about the movie offer and how much I wanted to play in that film and explained that I would lose only two months should things not work out the way I hoped.

He saw my point. I suspect that he may also have felt that his business could carry on without me and that my talents, whatever they were, would be better appreciated in the motion-picture industry than in a bank.

He called Papa and persuaded him to let me have a try at acting. Being a good businessman, he suggested certain changes in my contract and my father signed, rather reluctantly.

In the year 1921 the motion-picture business was not much different from what it is today. Unexpected delays, acts of God, uncompleted financing, the inability to get studio space and the right stars were a constant plague even then.

Sodom and Gomorrah was no exception. Our starting date was postponed again and again. It didn't bother me, as I was on full salary and able to spend that well-financed waiting period by leading the happy life of a playboy: sleeping late in the morning, dates for lunch, cocktails and dinner, and then to the theater, to bars and night clubs.

My father, who couldn't understand such a life of paid idleness, predicted that I would turn into a bum, a loafer, and a wastrel without purpose in life.

At long last work on the film began. On my first day of shooting, a limousine picked me up early in the morning and drove me to our shooting location.

I was made up, I got into my new clothes, and then I waited.

Waited for hours! Nothing was ready, and my only duty, besides waiting, was to see that my make-up was not spoiled and my clothes not wrinkled.

My first scene was simple: a carriage, drawn by two snow-white stallions, had to drive up and stop at a given point; I was to look out of the window, see my aged father (off camera), my face was to light up, and I was to get out and run to him with outstretched arms.

This scene we did eleven times. Twice the carriage overshot its mark, once it fell short of its mark, then I knocked off my hat while stepping out of the carriage, another time I tripped, the sun disappeared behind a cloud, my face didn't properly light up when seeing my aged father, the driver of the carriage picked his nose, the camera ran out of film, and the door handle broke off, leaving me undecided whether to keep it or throw it away.

After each unsuccessful take, the coachman had to drive his vehicle three hundred yards back around the bend, wait for his signal, and drive up again.

After each unsuccessful take, the fiery Hungarian temperament of Michael Kertesz got more fiery and more Hungarian. At first he muttered, then he hissed, then shouted, then yelled, and when one of our snow-white stallions dropped steaming, golden-brown horse apples right in front of the camera, he howled in agony.

We finally got the shot in the afternoon and knocked off for the day because the light was fading.

The film was jinxed from the start: two of our actors got sick, and all the film we had on them had to be reshot.

At the outskirts of the city, Sascha Film had erected, high on a hill, our biggest and most elaborate set: the Temple of Astarte. It was truly colossal, pyramid-shaped, terribly Assyrian in architecture, and about three hundred feet high.

In front of it was to be played the great climactic final scene of the film, when fire and brimstone rain from the heavens onto the principals and on about three thousand extras who would pretend to be fleeing and dying. And where Lot's wife turns into a pillar of salt because she couldn't resist a last peekaboo.

We had started shooting in front of that Babylonian atrocity and were leading up to the big scene.

That morning the car called for me early and on the way to our location picked up our star, Lucy Doraine and her director-husband Michael Kertesz (today better known as Mike Curtiz). We arrived at the Laarberg, the name of the hill on which stood our big set. We thought that the chauffeur had driven us to the wrong place, because at the dawn's early light no temple could be seen.

An old watchman walked over to us from the gate. "Some wind," he said pleasantly, and pointed to the horizon.

"What wind?" asked Mike.

"The north wind," explained an assistant, stickler for detail that he was, and with a large, sweeping gesture added: "Whoooosh! Biggest goddam north wind I ever saw."

We were too stunned to talk; even Mike was speechless. We got out of the car and surveyed the wreck: lumber, stucco and lots of painted cloth were all that was left of the Temple of Astarte.

Sascha Film was in too deep financially to call the whole thing off, so we finished all indoor scenes at the studio and postponed the exteriors for the following spring. Which meant that everyone on whom film had been shot was implored *please* to stay well, not to lose—or put on weight—and *especially* to stay alive. It also meant that we were paid full salary for the next thirty weeks, so we would be available in the month of May.

The prospect of my being idle for over half a year, while drawing a large salary which enabled me to grace the social scene as habitué of the theater, bars, and night clubs, was too much for Papa! He put his foot down; I had to go to work.

He begged his old friend Milan Reitler to please make room for me in his bank; good kind Milan gave me desk space and tried to keep me occupied with harmless little chores. His reluctance to burden me with responsibilities was fully matched by my reluctance to accept a position of trust. By that time I had already made up my mind that I preferred the world of celluloid to that of high finance and regarded the time spent in his office as a pleasant form of hibernation.

My main recollection of that highly respected banking establishment is that everybody was always very busy and that they employed some of the homeliest secretaries I have ever had the misfortune to see. Of course, that may have been one of the reasons why Reitler & Co. was so successful.

The telephone operator, a nice elderly lady, became my friend and confidante; I gave her a list of my current girl friends and my hangouts, and when Papa called me at the office to check if I was there, she made up wonderful stories why I wasn't at my desk and then got busy on the phone to locate and alert me.

"Bare winter suddenly was changed to spring," as the poet said—and the Temple of Astarte had been rebuilt in all its ugliness. I said good-by to Milan Reitler and was welcomed back at the Laarberg. Working on our picture *Sodom and Gomorrah* was a famous pyrotechnician and special-effects man called Wannemacher. A wonderful little man; on his right hand he had only two fingers, three on his left hand—the rest he had exploded away. And a piece of his nose was missing. But, undaunted by these little detonated misfortunes, he kept on handling explosives with great casualness—always with a lighted cigar in his mouth. During the first week of shooting he produced an earth slide. It was such a good earth-slide that he moved half a mountain far beyond the spot where he was supposed to let it slide. And partly buried the camera crew under the onrushing earth.

One of the scenes called for Lucy Doraine and me to

flee the holocaust of Sodom and Gomorrah. I had to carry her to the edge of a lake, place her on a float, push it off to the middle of the lake—when a "tremendous wave" was to rise and overturn the float. I was then to continue my heroic rescue operation through natatorial prowess.

Lucy, an experienced and therefore careful and suspicious lady of the cinema, asked who was to produce the "tremendous wave." When the name Wannemacher was mentioned, she paled.

He was called in and asked to explain what he intended to do. "Nothing to it," he said, waving his two-fingered hand. "I just placed a little can with black powder in the water and when the float glides over that spot, I'll ignite it and a little wave will come up." He smiled at our concern.

"I want to see the little wave before we shoot the scene," Lucy said pleasantly.

"Look here," said Mike with controlled impatience, "you're holding us up—the sun will be down in about an hour and we'll lose another shooting day!"

"I want to see the little wave," said Lucy, and sat down in her chair.

"Lucy—*darling*"—there was an undertone of danger in Mike's voice—"don't take advantage of the fact that we are married—be my good little baby girl—*get on that float!*"

The last was said through clenched teeth.

"I want to see the little wave," said Lucy in her smallest voice.

Mike walked away—muttering, and beating his head with his fists—but suddenly capitulated:

"All right—show her the goddam little wave!" The float was loaded with sandbags, approximating our combined weight, and pulled into position. Wannemacher, visibly wounded by Lucy's lack of confidence, walked over to the detonator box and confidently pushed down the lever. There was a rumble in the water, a deafening explosion, and a geyser of water rose seventy-five feet into the air.

When the column of water had collapsed and the smoke cleared, there was no more float, but for the next thirty seconds it rained kindling wood and bottom soil.

Wannemacher relit his cigar, which had been extinguished by the spray. "I guess I goofed," he chuckled. "I must have taken a can with dynamite instead of the black powder!"

Lucy rose and stalked Mike. We all stepped back to clear the ring. They stood, facing each other like a cobra and a mongoose. Then from both torrents of Hungarian burst forth. Unfortunately I know no Hungarian, except a few choice obscenities, but *these* I *heard!* Clearly, distinctly they stood out, articulated with frightening vigor.

A few years later Wannemacher crossed my path again. It was in Berlin: I played the title role in a film, *The Flagbearer of Sedan,* in which I won the Battle of Sedan single-handed, by waving a flag; which may be historically disputable, but was considered effective on the screen.

The day we shot the big battle we had twelve hundred extras—half of them dressed as Germans, vintage 1870, and the other half in French uniform. Artillery and cavalry were represented: ten cameras were mounted on high scaffolds, to photograph the battle from every angle. A tower had been erected for the director, from which he could guide the troops by yelling through a megaphone. Wardrobe men and women were running around, adjusting uniforms, a military expert went around, showing the extras how to carry a musket and making sure that the sabers and other military props were correctly hung and handled. Make-up men trimmed mustaches, laid on beards, and put on wigs.

In all this turmoil I saw a little man quietly smoking his

cigar. "Wannemacher," I asked, "WHAT ARE YOU DOING HERE?"

"Slezak, my boy"—his face lit up—"how are you—so nice to see you again—you look wonderf—"

"Don't change the subject," I interrupted. "I asked you what you are doing here? Not pyrotechnics by any chance?"

"Well, in a way—somehow—" He laughed gaily and his maimed hand pointed to hundreds of small mounds of earth that were visible on the "battlefield." "You see, my boy, out there I planted tiny toy torpedoes and when they go off there'll be a little smoke and that will give the effect of a shrapnel burst."

One of the assistants who had joined us and had listened to this description whispered to me:

"If one of these tiny toy torpedoes goes off while you are walking over it, you can look for a new job—in a harem—as chief eunuch."

That prospect made me swoon. "Wannemacher," I said with authority, "I want you to explode one of them for me."

"My dear boy"—he sounded sad—"don't you have any confidence in me?"

"NO" was my brutal reply.

At the demonstration a foot-long flame shot out of a puff of smoke.

That was all! It certainly looked harmless enough, but I refused to take chances. I had the director show me the exact route I had to walk and carefully noticed where in my path the little mounds of earth were planted.

The strategic planning of the battle was very simple: the two armies were to approach each other at the double and meet halfway in the field. The six hundred extras who represented the Germans were instructed to follow me—and at all times to stay *behind* me, so the heroic picture of me, waving the flag and leading them on to victory, would not be spoiled.

FIG. 1. ...lovely, gentle Mama! *(Pietzner)*

FIG. 2. Two dudes in Bavaria! *(E. Ganghofer)*

FIG. 3. Herr und Frau Kammersaenger! *(Mishkin Studio)*

FIG. 4. Mama and her brood *(Pietzner)*

FIG. 5. . . . en route to the Met!

FIG. 6. "Perfect harmony!" caricature by Enrico Caruso

Fig. 7. My locks were daily brushed and combed.
(Friedrich Kransfelder)

Fig. 8. . . . I hated them!

Fig. 9. The Lord of the Hunger Manor – and son!

Fig. 10. In Egern on the Tegernsee

Fig. 11. Our home in Vienna

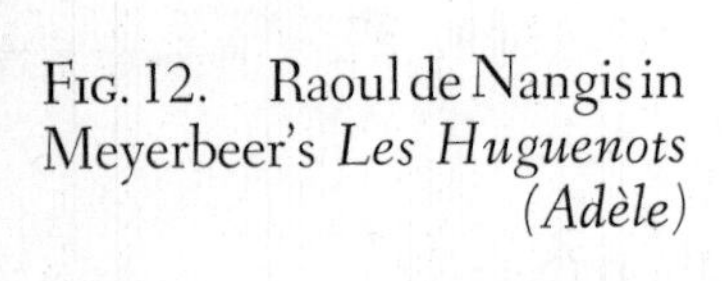

Fig. 12. Raoul de Nangis in Meyerbeer's *Les Huguenots* (*Adèle*)

Fig. 13. Tamino and Pamina (Emmy Destinn) in Mozart's *Magic Flute* (*Metropolitan Opera Archives*)

Fig. 14. My operatic debut (*Rudolf Jasky*)

Fig. 15. A really young "Jung-Siegfried" (*Hana Ltd.*)

Fig. 16. What time's the nex swan?

FIG. 17. Tannhäuser

FIG. 18. *Otello,* with Frances Alda, Florence Wickham, and Antonio Scotti
(*Metropolitan Opera Archives*)

Fig. 19. The Duke of Mantua, disguised as a student (*Rafael*)

Fig. 20. *Le Prophète* by Meyerbeer (*Raphael*)

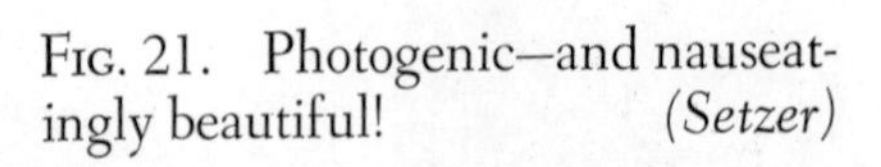

Fig. 21. Photogenic—and nauseatingly beautiful! (*Setzer*)

FIG. 22. Hans-Heinz or Horst-Juergen! *(U F A)*

FIG. 23. Pure innocent about to be seduced by vamp *(Terra Film)*

FIG. 24. 103 pounds ago (*Glogau*)

FIG. 25. (*RKO*)

Fig. 26. 102 pounds ago *(Glogau)*

Fig. 27. *(RKO)*

Fig. 28. Young devil!

Fig. 29. Somewhat older devil (*RKO*)

Fig. 30. . . . God kissed me on both eyes

Fig. 31. My brood: Erika, Leo, Ingrid (*Peter Basch*)

FIG. 32. The master of Redhill Farm *(Associated Press)*

FIG. 33. Leo, who suggested using paper and pencil *(Peter Basch)*

The alert was given: we all lined up—the director on his tower fired a shot—and off we went. The French came running and we ran toward them, with me and my flag in the lead, but every time I came within ten feet of a mound, I marked time, marching furiously in one spot, six hundred men behind me doing the same, until the tiny toy torpedo exploded, then I rushed forward again in another spurt, until I came to the next unexploded mound; there I marked time again. These stops I covered up with acting, ferociously swinging the flag and yelling at the top of my voice:

"Follow me, men—follow the flag—on to victory!"

The director on his tower was close to apoplexy—he bellowed and screamed into his megaphone for me to go ahead, but I wouldn't budge as long as I saw danger on the ground.

The Germans had barely covered a hundred fifty yards when the French were upon us. My only concern in the melee was to hold the flag high enough for the camera to see. Assistants swarmed around the side lines and made the French retreat and we won the Battle of Sedan.

Next day in the projection room the big boss of our film company saw the film we had shot:

"Excellent idea," he beamed, "to have the French exhaust themselves by running against that slowly advancing wall of Germans. Ingenious directorial touch!"

Our director, I am ashamed to report, nodded in agreement and accepted the accolade with appropriate modesty.

Sodom and Gomorrah was drawing to its close. The scene that was to be shot last was the Temple of Astarte collapsing and—in crashing—burying the pagan idols of the false god.

Everybody connected with the Austrian film industry was there to watch the event: friends, relatives, even the directors of the bank who had financed the film. Tension was high.

Wannemacher had spent several weeks setting charges

under all supports and made a last check. All was ready! He and his helpers stood poised, holding the levers of the detonator boxes.

Mike Curtiz gave the signal!

All levers were pressed down simultaneously!

Smoke appeared: the temple trembled, rose a few feet in the air, swayed, and settled gently back to where it had been standing.

Agonizing silence reigned!

Mike Curtiz threw himself on the floor, babbling, groaning, and grunting.

Arnold Pressburger rattled: "No–NO–NOOO," each NO louder than the last and more exasperated.

The financiers completely lost their corporate dignity; they rose as a group and turned on Wannemacher—like a school of deadly piranha attacking a floating corpse.

But all he said was: "I am as surprised as you are!"

In spite of all the trouble and delays *Sodom and Gomorrah* became a big success.

"Let me have your passport," Papa said after I had arrived in Tegernsee. I handed it to him, and he slipped it in his pocket.

"And now, my dear Walter!"—he spoke quietly and with great determination—"as of this minute, your career as an actor is *ended!* Until such time as you are of age, I *alone* will determine what you will do. You are going into industry. You will report at the Primus Paper Company in Beuel on September first." He walked to his study, ducked under the low doorframe, and closed it.

I was thunderstruck! I ran after him, but Mama stopped me: "Please don't argue with Papa," she begged. "Try to see why he is doing that; after all, during the last ten months you spent only seventy-three days working, *if* one can call that work—the rest of the time you loafed. What kind of a life is that for a young man, what kind of a future—"

"I will not work in a paper factory," I interrupted, "I will not be dictated what profession to choose—I am a film actor, and I will remain a film actor."

"Oh no, you won't!" Papa stuck his head out of the door. "I have written letters to all film companies in Austria and Germany, informing them that you are underage and that I will sue them should they dare to offer you a job. You are going to Beuel and that's final." He slammed the door.

"All right," I yelled, "I'll go to Beuel, but I won't do an hour's work there, and I will inform them so when I arrive. You'll just have to support me until I am twenty-one years old and *then* I will be a movie actor."

"In that case, my dear Walter"—Papa plunged out of his room again—"I'll go to court and arrange that you'll be declared a minor until you are twenty-four!"

He drew himself up to his full height of six feet seven, made a triumphant about-face to re-enter his room, and crashed head on against the low beam of the door.

He cried out in pain, Mama rushed to him. "Now see what you've done!" And she began to cry.

A welt the size of a large hot dog began to grow on Papa's forehead; he looked at me, still stunned from the collision, and said in a hollow voice:

"You made your mother cry."

The next weeks weren't pleasant ones. Papa was stubborn and hurt that his authority had been challenged.

I was just as stubborn and determined to get my way. But all my life I hated scenes, domestic and otherwise, so, to avoid them, I went on long mountain-climbing and hiking trips.

O, my grandmother, always listening at doors and, full

of gossip, filled me in on every detail: the Primus Company was selected for two reasons: 1. My brother-in-law was on the board of directors and, 2. Beuel, where it was located, was one of the smallest, dullest towns in the Rhineland, populated by staid and solid burghers and with absolutely no night life of any sort. O also told me that she had overheard my father say: "Let the boy stew for a while, when he sees that I am not giving in, he'll come around."

How little he knew me!

On August 18 I wrote a birthday poem for Papa. It was in the form of a petition: A medieval serf begs his all-powerful lord and master for an audience and a chance to plead his case "without being interrupted, without being yelled at, without tantrums, without threats of decapitation or exile into the pulp mines of the Rhineland."

Papa listened in silence and looked deeply offended. Mama was aghast. "You have ruined the whole day for him," she whispered.

But during the big ceremonial meal, I watched him attacking his food with earnest concentration and joyful enthusiasm. I may have ruined his day, but certainly not his appetite.

The next morning he came to my room. "Want to go fishing with me?" he asked rather casually. Out in the boat he suddenly said: "Go ahead, plead your case, I won't interrupt you!"

And I talked, talked like never before. I guess I said all the clichés about wanting to lead my own life, about making my own way, like he had done, about my enthusiasm for acting, about the great future the movie industry offered. He listened attentively and said: "I'll talk it over with Mama."

That same night, they gave me permission to go to Berlin, then the center of the film industry, for a year and try my luck there. He even agreed to finance me and loaned me a thousand marks. It was the only time he gave me money, and I paid half of it back.

I arrived in Berlin with two letters of recommendation: one to Max Reinhardt, and the other to a very famous actor, Paul Wegener, who was a star both in the theater and in films.

I knew that actors are notoriously late risers, so I didn't present myself until twelve-thirty. Lyda Salmonova, a celebrated dancer and at that time the wife of the oft-married Wegener, received me graciously, said her husband would be right down, asked me to wait, and disappeared in a cloud of purple musk. Two and a half hours later in staggered a man, a wild look on his Mongol-featured face, hair disheveled, exhaling alcohol fumes.

"Who the hell are you?" he asked rudely, and then, full of suspicion, added: "How did you get in here?"

I quickly presented my letter. He tried to focus on it but couldn't quite make it and handed it back to me. "You read it," he commanded.

When I had finished, he beamed and slapped his thighs. "Good old Leo, the singing sea elephant," he roared. He belched and let himself fall into a chair. For fully two minutes he stared at the carpet. Then he looked up. "What do you want?" he growled.

"I am an actor, and I would like to get your advice on—"

"You are an actor," he shouted, and catapulted himself out of his chair. "You've come to the right place, my boy. I have good advice for you, real good advice—" He stood in front of me, gently swaying, and after another long pause he put his arm around my shoulder and said very confidentially:

"DON'T EVER MARRY—no matter WHAT they tell you—don't EVER marry!"

I said, "Thank you very much," picked up Papa's letter, and left.

My visit to Max Reinhardt was even less successful; the doorman at the Deutsches Theater took my letter, walked up a flight of stairs, and when he came back he informed me that Herr Professor would get in touch with me.

He never did.

At that time, the motion-picture industry had no agents, at least I didn't know of any, so the telephone directory became my guide. I had myself photographed in several alluring poses and distributed these freely to sundry doormen and assistant secretaries. But I was never able to get my foot in the door of one single director or producer. They were too well protected.

One night I went to the Restaurant Schwanecke, a gathering place for show folks. I was alone, holding my glass of beer, and was overawed because at the table next to mine there happened to be sitting nearly all the greats of the German movie industry. Emil Jannings, Conrad Veidt, with his wife Gussy Holl, (who a few years later married Emil Jannings), Ernst Lubitsch, the great director, Pola Negri, *and* Lyda Salmonova. I tried very hard to catch her eye, but she never looked in my direction. Jannings became aware of my efforts and nudged her:

"Lyda, that child over there is trying to flirt with you!" All eyes turned to me, and I turned crimson. "How sweet, he is blushing," said Pola Negri, with her heavy Polish accent. But Lyda Salmonova remembered me, and I was invited over to their table.

I was floating on waves of happiness and couldn't believe my good luck. I instantly developed a mad crush on Pola Negri, but I am sad to have to report that it was never reciprocated.

Jannings was especially nice; he invited me to his house, made a few telephone calls, and managed to get me the second lead in a film starring Harry Liedtke, a famous matinee idol.

Two days before shooting was to begin, the lawyer of the film company got me on the phone. "I am sorry to inform you, Mr. Slezak, that the contract you signed with us is null and void; it seems that you are still underage and we have a letter from your father—"

"But he rescinded that. He gave his permission, I assure you."

"In that case, we shall require a notarized letter signed by your father to that effect. Please have that letter in my office not later than three o'clock this afternoon!"

"PLEASE don't hire another actor," I begged. "Papa is somewhere on a concert tour, but I will try to find him as quickly as I can." I was frantic.

"I am terribly sorry, but we can't wait. The picture starts in two days, and we will have to make other arrangements. Better luck next time." And he hung up.

I called Emil Jannings, but he was somewhere on location and couldn't be reached. Two days later, I got hold of Papa in Stuttgart. "Get the list of the film companies to whom you have written," I begged him, "and tell them that now I am allowed to be an actor."

But the list was somewhere in his desk in Tegernsee, so he sent me a "To whom it may concern" letter, properly signed and notarized, but unfortunately four days too late.

Soon after that, the picture *Sodom and Gomorrah* was released in Berlin and—pronto—I got another job: the romantic lead opposite Lucie Mannheim. The two other male parts were played by two of the greatest actors of the German stage and films, Heinrich George and Werner Krauss.

My first scene was with these two champions. It was a difficult scene, and we rehearsed again and again. I felt that I was hopelessly outmatched, and the more we rehearsed the worse I got. Suddenly the director called a halt, took me aside:

"I am afraid we are wasting time," he said sympathetically. "You just won't do; I have to let you go."

I was close to tears. "You don't give me a real chance," I wailed. "That's not fair . . ."

Suddenly Werner Krauss stood there, grabbed me by the shoulders, and shook me. "How dare you say we are not fair," he hissed. "What right have *you* to presume to be in the same scene with Heinrich George and myself—so far you are nothing but a pretty boy amateur, you don't know the first thing about acting, you don't know how to talk, how to walk. Go away—learn your trade, and don't try to begin at the top!" He released me. "Now run along, kid," he said gruffly, "and come back when you're no longer an apprentice. *Then,* we'll be glad to have you."

He turned to the director. "Now let's get an *actor* for the part."

I don't know how I got home that day; I was so humiliated, so ashamed. But later in the evening I wrote a letter to Werner Krauss, asking him what he thought I should do. "First learn to speak and get a job in a good theater in the provinces and get experience," he wrote back.

The next morning I enrolled in the studio of Professor Daniel, the famous diction coach! And every day for three hours I recited the German equivalent of "How now, brown cow."

One more opportunity came my way: Ossi Oswalda, a famous film comedienne whose career had been started by Ernst Lubitsch, hired me as her leading man.

At the first day of shooting I was as nervous as only an actor can be who knows that *this* time he has to make good. In the first scene I had to be gay, jaunty, and debonair. But

I couldn't get rid of a fixed smile that desperately clung to my face, and I had no co-ordination left; each limb was independently debonair and jaunty. They tried the scene again and again, with great patience, but at the day's end, I was again taken aside. "We are wasting time, you don't have enough experience . . . !"

I made up my mind to commit suicide. On the way to the parking lot I talked to a well-known dancing star who was working on another picture. I told her of my decision. She took me to her house. And after forty-eight hours she had convinced me that life was worth living.

But my money was running out, and I was too proud to ask Papa for more. In fact, I hadn't even told him about my two flops. He still thought I was doing the film with Werner Krauss.

The news that I had been fired twice in a row spread fast and was recounted as a good joke. Emil Jannings was quite calm about it. "Someday I'll tell you how I began, how many times I lost parts, and how hard it was for me to get to the top."

He also thought it a good idea for me to go to the provinces for a few years of training. But that I regarded as a complete defeat. I wanted to stay and make a success in Berlin.

At that time a pattern of my life that has blessedly stayed with me up to now began to evolve.

Every time I set my cap for a certain goal and work hard to get it, it's in vain. But suddenly I will stumble and fall on my face! And when I rise, I see a shining piece of completely unexpected good luck lying there, begging to be picked up.

Such a shiny piece of good luck, completely out of left field, blinked at me one drizzly Saturday morning. I was sitting on a bench in the Tiergarten. The night before I had been locked out of my room because I couldn't pay my back rent, and all my suits, shirts, and shoes were held as hostages.

An elderly gentleman with a dog on a leash walked by; the dog barked furiously at me; he, too, disliked actors. The man looked at me:

"Aren't you Leo Slezak's boy?" He sounded amazed. It was an old friend of Papa's, Gustav Charlé, a theatrical producer. He sat down and looked me over quizzically; only then did I realize that I must have looked like a bum, uncombed, unshaven, and disheveled.

"Are you in trouble?" he asked. I nodded.

"Did you steal anything?" I shook my head: No.

"Are you hungry?" I nodded.

"Come along!" He took me to his house. I had breakfast, a bath; he said: "Have a good sleep and later on we'll talk."

Gustav Charlé at that time had a hit show running in Berlin, *Dorine and the Chance,* a comedy with music, and that evening he invited me to the theater. It was a charming little play, only five men and one woman were in the cast, and a young performer named Harold Paulsen was the success of the show as a dancing *buffo.*

That night events telescoped like a fabulous surrealistic dream; it was unbelievable, hectic, and wonderful: Right after the show, Harold Paulsen broke his leg! He didn't have an understudy! Charlé worked with me most of the night; I memorized the part; on Sunday I learned the music, which was easy —all patter songs that did not require any voice; the choreographer taught me the dances; all day Monday I rehearsed with the cast. Mrs. Charlé went to my lodgings and bailed out my clothes and at eight-thirty the curtain rose.

Dressed in tails, wearing a top hat, a cane loosely tucked under my arm, I sauntered down to the footlights, a picture of relaxed elegance. On cue I cakewalked across the stage singing the immortal lines of my opening couplet:

"In ev'ry bar there sits a gent.
To ev'ry damsel he's a friend,
To every one, who, quite risqué,
Displays a low cut décol'té!"

As this song was considered daring and the character I was portraying quite a devil, I was surprised to hear laughter. I became flustered and looked down to Mrs. Charlé, who sat in the first row. Horror was written all over her face. She frantically pointed at me and then on downward. I followed her gaze: my fly was wide open, gaping, grinning at the customers.

I turned my back to the audience, continued with my song and dance and *buttoned* and *buttoned* and *buttoned!*

When I faced my public again, some funny, funny man out front applauded. The house came down with laughter. From that day on, I considered myself adorable on-stage.

I stayed with the Dorine Company for the rest of the season. In the month of May, I embarked on a tour of the Netherlands with a new play, *Jugend,* and an especially luscious leading lady.

On the day of the opening in The Hague, I called for her at her hotel to escort her to the theater. Her phone didn't answer, so I went up to her room. When I opened the door, I first thought a horrible crime had been committed. She was lying on the floor, wearing nothing but a few hairpins, but was, as I soon realized, stone drunk and out cold.

Our opening at The Hague was an important kickoff for the rest of our tour through Holland, and we were all on a "share the spoils basis," so I rolled up my sleeves and went to work.

I dumped her into the bathtub. Then I turned on the shower, alternately ice cold and red hot, I ordered strong coffee from room service and forced her to drink it, I walked her around the room for half an hour, then I shoved a pair of shoes over her feet, threw a coat around her, pushed her into a taxi, and delivered her to the theater. By then she was fairly sober, but she didn't want to go on, because her hair was still wet and she looked like a drowned mouse. So we wrapped different kinds of cloth around her head and she played the whole show wearing turbans.

Being basically a fine trouper, she gave an excellent performance and our show went over big.

After the last curtain call, our producer ordered me to take her back to the hotel and make sure that she stayed off the sauce. So I baby-sat with that luscious lush. She told me her sad and tragic story—all in baby talk.

It seemed that for the last year and a half she was "keeping company" with a rich old merchant prince who had made his money in ladies' underwear.

"Do you know what I call him?" she asked me, with big googoo eyes.

"No, I don't," I answered, able to contain my curiosity.

"I'll tell you what I call him," she sniveled in a tiny voice. "I call him PAPPI!"

"Why, that's sweet," I said.

"Yes, it is." She began to cry. "Pappi is *sooo* good to me, he buys *aall* my furs and *aaalll* my clothes and *aaaallll* my jewels! And he pays *aaaallll* my bills. And now—now, that goddam stupid idiot maid of mine passed on *all* my bills to him, passed them on while I was *away,* before I had a chance to *check* them! And Pappi got the bills for the suits and shirts and shoes and ties and *everything* I bought for Paul!" she was now howling like a road-company Medea and threw herself on the bed, beating the pillows with her fists.

"Here—look—read—" she sobbed, and handed me the letter she had received that morning.

In it Pappi announced the breaking off of all relations,

diplomatic and otherwise, and immediate severance of all financial aid, lend lease, and/or other forms of subsidy.

He also let it be known that he had invaded her apartment in Berlin and had repossessed whatever furs, jewels, and other tokens of his infatuation he had donated and which she, trusting little soul that she was, had foolishly left behind when she went off to Holland.

It was quite a letter, and I could well understand that these revelations had driven her to the bottle.

Around 3 A.M. she regained her initiative and called Pappi long distance. I sat there, listening fascinated and in awe of female virtuosity: she cajoled, denied, explained, made up fantastic lies; lies so outrageous that they sounded almost true; how Paul had used her charge account, how she hated him and would never speak to him again; how she was always being maligned and the victim of misunderstandings: remember the time a man's pajama was found in her bedroom, and it was all a laundry mix-up? In the end, she made Pappi apologize for having unjustly accused her, and she ordered him to come to Holland by the next train to ask her forgiveness.

Right after she had hung up, she made another call to Paul; she told him how much she missed and loved him and promised to pay the next installment on his sports car.

Then she felt fine, and I ordered a bottle of champagne, which took quite some doing, because it was nearly four in the morning. We celebrated her victory.

Pappi arrived two days later, laden with valuable gifts, and we all gave him a hero's welcome.

All during the war and in the years following it, food rationing and frugality were constantly with everyone in Austria and Germany. So Holland was paradise.

The day I found out that one could go to a restaurant and order anything one's heart desired—that was the day I ate eleven portions of whipped cream with powdered sugar in one sitting. I had not tasted that since 1914.

I went on regular food exploration trips. In a fish smokery I was taught how to gormandize young eels. The skin is pulled off like the cover of an umbrella; the eel is then held by its head and its tail; stretched, and—in the manner reminiscent of eating corn on the cob—the tender meat is licked and sucked off.

Niewe haring, so sweet they taste like candy, are eaten via hand-to-mouth route on every street corner.

And, of course, there are *Poffertjes:* little pancakes, about an inch and a half in diameter, made in specially designed cast-iron trays with recessed round molds, and eaten piping hot with lots of butter and sugar.

In Holland I fell in with a group of young artists who awakened my interest in painting. The overwhelming beauty of the treasures that are housed at the Rijks Museum in Amsterdam and at the Mauritshuis in The Hague made a deep impression on me. A few of the Rembrandts, Vermeers, and Jan Steens on their walls have become dear friends; I visit them whenever I have a chance to go to that wonderful little country.

Bearing a set of glowing notices about my performance, all written in Dutch and therefore open to various interpretations, I arrived in Tegernsee and was able to erase the last bastion of doubt Papa still entertained about my becoming a mummer and strolling player, dedicated to a life of grease paint behind footlights.

But he fully agreed with Emil Jannings and Werner Krauss that I should learn my trade in the provinces.

The theater in Europe is set up quite differently from ours here in America. Here an entrepreneur gets hold of a script that shows promise; he then approaches financiers—to provide the money—they are called "angels," presumably because they so rarely receive any rewards for their good deeds; he then hires a director and stage designer and picks the exact types of actors he feels are right for the parts; then he goes to John Shubert and begs for a theater. And if he is lucky (his chances are about 3 per cent) he has a hit that will run several years.

If he is not lucky (97-per-cent probability) the thing closes after a very short while, the "angels" lose their money and write the loss off their income taxes, and the hapless, poor actors look for other employment.

That system makes it possible for great stars such as Katharine Cornell, Helen Hayes, Judith Anderson, Maurice Evans, and many others to be without a Broadway play for three or four years in a row, or until a vehicle that fits their specialized talents comes around again.

No stage actor in America ever has a position!

At best he has a job!

In Europe, on the other hand, practically every small town has its municipal or civic theater that plays repertory on a year-round basis and hires actors for two or three years. According to their looks, age, and special talents, they are classified as juveniles, ingénues, characters, comedians, elegant and dramatic leading ladies. They must know the classic as well as the modern repertory and be able to play Romeo one day and young Marchbanks the next night. Thus they get established and become "beloved" and box-office draws.

Casting for the fall season is usually done in February or March, and by the time I arrived from Holland, all vacancies for a romantic juvenile were filled. But Papa managed to get me a contract with the municipal theater in Chemnitz, an unattractive industrial town in the province of Saxony.

The Herr Director of that theater was Herr Tauber, the father of the celebrated Richard Tauber.

The train that carried me into Chemnitz arrived at dawn.

It was a gray foggy morning and a heavy blanket of soot and smog hung over the town. I waited at the railway station until ten o'clock and then went to the theater to see Mr. Tauber. An unpleasant, sullen young assistant received me.

"The Herr Director sees actors only on Wednesdays and Fridays from ten to eleven and from three to four. I'll put your name down for an appointment."

He handed me a list of lodgings whose landladies were broad-minded enough to rent to actors, and I was dismissed.

The dwellings I inspected were all the same: crummy, squalid, cheerless, and furnished with exceptional ugliness. But by late afternoon I was too tired to care and dropped my bags in an unfriendly, badly ventilated room that received its trickle of daylight from a courtyard. I had to pay one month's rent in advance, so I was trapped. I was miserable, depressed, and discouraged.

But the following day was Wednesday, and I was eager to find out what exciting roles Mr. Tauber had lined up for me.

"As you probably know, I hired you only as a favor to your father," he began. "All my plays for the season are cast, but we may use you as a stand-by in case somebody gets sick. And we will try to find some small parts for you." He walked me to the door. "My assistant will give you your contract and your first role. Good-by!"

I was too stunned to protest.

The contract they handed me read: "Beginner in the first year."! *Beginner in the first year,* I, who had played a star part in a Berlin theater, I, who had thrilled thousands of Hollanders with my renditions of "In ev'ry bar there sits a gent." *I,* a beginner in the first year?

The role that was to mark my debut in Chemnitz was that of a detective. He had exactly two lines to say: "We have to search the room" and "Nothing, no trace of him."

I rushed back to Mr. Tauber's office but was brusquely stopped and had to apply for another appointment the following week.

I brooded revenge for such humiliation and resolved to make those provincial clowns sit up and take notice of me.

The play in which I was to show off my talents to the people of Chemnitz was a very serious affair. During rehearsals I said my two lines with quiet authority. The director didn't think that I looked believable as a detective, so he told me to stick on a mustache to make me appear older.

Came opening night: the entrance of the detective was the dramatic high point of the second act: Will he or will he not find the hero-criminal, who is being hidden by the lovely lady of the mansion, the very one he tries to rob? When I came on-stage, my face was garnished with a large, funny red nose and by a huge walrus mustache that all but covered my mouth and chin. A ripple of mirth went through the audience; I opened my mouth and stuttered: "Wwww-eee haave tttoo sssssearch th-th-the rrrooom—" Laughter greeted that line. The poor lovely lady of the mansion said through clenched teeth: "Please do your duty!" whereupon I opened a small drawer in a desk, looked inside, and said:

"N-o-o-t-th-ing, n-n-n-ooo t-t-t-r-r-a-a-c-c-e of hi-i-m," clicked my heels, turned around, walked into a lamp, knocked it down, and exited, tripping over the threshold. I heard laughter and scattered applause and returned the false nose and walrus mustache to the make-up department, where I had "borrowed" it.

The door to my dressing room burst open like an explosion, and framed Mr. Tauber, head lowered, pawing the ground like an attacking rhino:

"You, you, are you *mad?* You know what you've *done?*" The words shot out of him like ugly puffs of smoke belching out of a locomotive going uphill. "You've *ruined* the play! The people are *laughing*! *Laughing*, do you hear?"

"I am very sorry, Herr Director." I remained dignified. "But *that* was my interpretation of such a tiny, insignificant role!"

"Somebody *stop* me," he panted, "somebody *please* stop me before I *kill* the little son of a bitch."

As nobody seemed willing to stop him, and I feared that a lynching mob might assemble any minute, I fled the premises.

Surprisingly, Mr. Tauber didn't throw me out! The following morning I was called to his office and given the biggest bawling out of my life. I pretended to be overwhelmed by remorse and he, good kind soul that he was, grew mellow and generous:

"All right, Slezak," he growled, "I'll give you one more chance; now I want that clearly understood—just *one* more chance: I'll let you play Brother Dominic in *Drifting Souls*. But this time no horseplay!"

I rushed out of his office. "I am going to play Brother Dominic," I told the unfriendly assistant. "Please give me the play."

I rushed home and began scanning the script: page after page I turned, but no "Brother Dominic." Then, toward the end of Act III, I read:

(A BLUE SPOTLIGHT SUDDENLY REVEALS THE VISION OF A MONK, HIS DEATH SKULL PARTLY HIDDEN BY COWL AND HOOD. HE RAISES HIS SKELETON HAND AND SPEAKS WITH SEPULCHRAL VOICE:)

BROTHER DOMINIC

"Gunther, you evil one, I have returned, I—"

(GUNTHER CRIES OUT IN ANGUISH)

"Brother Dominic!"

BROTHER DOMINIC

"I curse you, curse you, curse you . . ."

(THE VOICE TRAILS OFF AND THE APPARITION VANISHES.)

That was all. *That* was the part! Gunther yakked on with a four-page monologue, recalling all his dastardly sins, and stabbed himself. *Curtain.*

Well, Chemnitz was definitely not the place for me, that much was now very clear. The young actors whose roles I coveted were a sturdy group, brimming over with health and strength, and it seemed too much of a long shot to waste a whole year on the possibility of another broken leg.

Nevertheless, I attended all rehearsals for *Drifting Souls.*

On the day of the première, an elaborate make-up job was applied to my face. It converted it into a grinning death mask. But as I sat in my dressing room, waiting for my entrance in Act III, the goddess of mischief appeared and sneaked a glorious idea into my brain!

When my cue approached, I slipped on my cowl and pulled the hood tightly over my face. In my hand I held a bony skeleton hand. In complete darkness I stepped out of the wings onto the stage, where only the small area where Gunther sat at a desk was dimly lit. I pulled back my hood.

I had removed the death-mask make-up from the left side of my face, the one that was turned away from the audience. In its stead I had painted the face of a lovely juvenile, with *one* red cheek, *one* graceful eyebrow, and *half* a rosebud lip.

A ghostlike blue light came up on me and I raised the bony hand; in sepulchral voice my first line rang out:

"Gunther, you evil one, I have returned, I—"

Gunther looked up and saw me: his well-rehearsed cry of anguish turned into a gurgle. He tried to collect himself, but the more he tried, the harder he was shaking with hysterical laughter.

"I curse you, curse you, curse you . . ." I continued, but all that came out of him were choked convulsions. So he took the easy way out; he "stabbed himself," skipping his entire monologue about his dastardly sins. They had to ring down the curtain.

By the time they got to me, cold cream had already removed both half faces: the death mask and the lovely juvenile. I was glistening with innocence.

To be thrown out is always unpleasant, even if it was provoked. So when the call came to see the big boss for what I knew would be the final reckoning, I felt pretty pale around the gills.

Mr. Tauber's office was on the second floor of the old theater building and had to be reached by a circular staircase; at the foot of that staircase stood the mail rack, and as I hurried up the steps I noticed that there were several letters lying in the section marked S.

Two of them were for me!

One from Vienna and one from Berlin. I had to read them twice before the news sank in. But then my gills instantly changed color, my step became buoyant, and my manner assured. I opened the door to Mr. Tauber's office: he sprang up from his desk and rushed out of his corner like a prize fighter moving in for the kill. He drew a deep breath, but before he could get started, I stopped him:

"My dear Herr Director, let's not lose our tempers! I know that you are not happy with me and, frankly, I am not happy at your theater, so I came to ask for my release!"

"Release? What do you mean release?"—the color of his face turned navy blue—"I am firing you, you little snotty presumptuous—"

"PLEASE, Herr Director, let's not have a scene." I was

all calmness and superiority. "The fact is that I have already made some other arrangements. First I plan a guest appearance in the play *Dorine and the Chance* at the Buergertheatre in Vienna, and after that, I will star in a picture at UFA in Berlin!"

Mr. Tauber was completely deflated. He stared at me, eyes wide open, the lower part of his lip hanging down on his chin. "I don't understand it," he said in a small voice. "If one can make guest appearances in Vienna, why does one come to Chemnitz in the first place?"

The invitation to play in Vienna came from Gustav Charlé and was a bona fide offer.

But the letter from UFA was just an invitation to make a screen test for the title role in one of their elite productions, a film called *Michael.* What difference did that make? I was so intoxicated with hope and confidence, so overwhelmed by this new turn of Fortune's wheel that I knew I couldn't fail.

Never had I been so happy to leave a town! At the railway station, I walked all the way up to the front of the train that was to remove me from Chemnitz. There I patted the locomotive and kissed the engineer.

My test for *Michael* turned out well, and I was signed. The director was the famous Carl Theodor Dreyer, who later became world renowned for his film *Joan of Arc.*

Sinclair Lewis once said to me: "My teacher of literature at Yale insisted that I had no future as a writer. I became a novelist only to prove him wrong."

There is wisdom in that facetious quip. I believe that everybody has a few special people in his life to whom he wants to prove that he has made good. For me, these people were my parents. So when I walked in on them with a contract for the star part with the most important motion-picture company in Europe, I felt happy and proud and vindicated.

And it was so wonderful to be back again, in my old room, in the clean environment of our home.

Several times, in later years, when I was on the verge of marrying some beautiful, exciting creature, the thought "How would she fit in at our home, could she give me the same atmosphere I know and love so much?" usually dampened my ardor and in the end stopped me from making a mistake.

I was aware of the risk I took in stepping out on a stage in Vienna as the fledgling son of Leo Slezak. But as my singing was negligible and my main talent at that time lay in my dancing, I knew that I would be able to bear the inevitable comparison with Papa. One critic wrote: "His father's talent has slipped into his feet." At the time I was very offended; today I think it's a compliment.

I started my engagement at UFA in the fall of 1924. Berlin was then the most exciting, the most alive, the most productive, and by far the most immoral city in Europe. Inflation was at its peak, money had no longer any real value, employees who got paid at noon and rushed to the bank found that their salaries had diminished 20 per cent within the hour. A ride on a streetcar would cost a hundred fifty million German marks one day and five hundred million the next. The people whose livelihood depended upon annuities and fixed incomes were wiped out and had to sell their belongings piece by piece.

The few crumbs of financial intelligence that had clung to my memory during my apprenticeship at the bank and the stock exchange now began to bear fruit. When I negotiated my contract with UFA, I demanded and they agreed to pay my salary in U.S. dollars.

Never before or after that had I been that rich! I lived

in a lavish three-room apartment in a villa in the best section of the town. My monthly rent was *two dollars,* and the landlady considered herself very fortunate because I paid her these two dollars in American currency.

My natural greedy instinct was to use all my surplus and buy up real estate, but a friend of Papa's, an international banker, warned me against it. He predicted that after the German mark had been stabilized a law would be passed that retroactively revaluated all sales of real estate, and would compel the buyers to pay the difference between the purchase price and the assessed real value, plus interest on the whole sum.

And that few people would be in a position to do that and lose everything.

There is a story that bears credence. At that time Douglas Fairbanks, Sr., tried to buy Austria.

It was well within his means as a dollar millionaire! He never could understand why they wouldn't sell it to him.

As there was no point in saving worthless money, people spent every million mark they made with reckless abandon.

The theaters and arts flourished like never before—three opera houses played ten months a year. Besides the standard repertory of Wagner, Puccini, Gounod, etc., all the "moderns" were performed. Franz Schreker's *Die Gezeichneten, Der Schatzgraeber,* Paul Hindemith's *Cardillac,* Stravinsky's *Petrouchka,* the works by Richard Strauss and Hans Pfitzner, Ernst Křenek's *Leben des Orest* and *Jonny Spielt Auf,* and in 1925, Alban Berg's *Wozzeck* exploded on the Berlin scene and caused furious and heated polemics.

The theater reached its highest level, Max Reinhardt, Leopold Jessner, Karl Heinz Martin, Erwin Piscator were its guiding spirits; new playwrights like Ernst Toller, Ferdinand Bruckner, and Bertolt Brecht got their first hearings.

Friedrich Hollaender, who helped our divine Marlene win world acclaim with his song "Falling in Love Again," which he wrote for the film *Der Blaue Engel,* ran an outstanding political cabaret where every sham and every cliché, every public figure's phoniness was exposed, attacked, and cut down to size.

A flood of survivors of the Russian Revolution had poured into Berlin, and many of them—somehow they all claimed to be grand dukes and grand duchesses—found employment as doormen and ladies'-room attendants in the innumerable night clubs that had sprung up like mushrooms. Little dingy cellar joints and the great plush Trocadero, where every table was equipped with a telephone from which you could call every other table in the room, were packed every night with profiteers and manipulators of foreign currency. The Eldorado night club, where female impersonators and transvestites performed, was patronized by homosexuals and curious tourists and operated openly under the benevolent eye of the police.

The economic upheaval of inflation had driven many women into prostitution, and they bluntly advertised in the newspapers under the thin guise of "massage salons." Wild parties that usually ended in orgies were commonplace daily occurrences and dope pushers and addicts had a field day. I still marvel at my good luck that I managed to come out of this period unscarred, relatively pure, and normal.

I was considered a matinee idol because I was photogenic and nauseatingly beautiful.

A well-known magazine, *The Uhu,* published an article, "What is manly beauty?" and to illustrate their point, they printed photos of Rudolph Valentino, Antonio Moreno, and . . . me. My mother bought twenty-seven copies.

My movie career ran in cycles of three groups of stories:

I. Innocent pure young man is seduced by alluring vamp, prevented from throwing away his life by father, who makes financial settlement with alluring vamp, then takes up with vamp himself, but *only* to prove to his son what a worthless creature he, the son, has been squandering his finest emotions on. The vamp was usually played by Lya de Putti.

II. Naval cadet, usually named Guenther-Jochen or some other double first name, serves on same battleship that had once been commanded by his late hero-father. Guenther-Jochen doesn't believe hero's death for the Fatherland to be proudest aim man can have. Is therefore considered coward and disgrace to memory of old Herr Kapitaen, whose picture stares down from the wall of the officers' mess, an inspiration to all. On shore leave, meets young naval nurse; she spurns him as unworthy of his family tradition and the uniform he wears. Guenther-Jochen instantly begins to drip with remorse, sneaks into officers' mess and has monologue (in subtitles) with painting of Herr Kapitaen. Following morning he starts to commit great feats of bravery which instantly make him eligible for hero's death and burial with full military honors at sea, his body wrapped in a German flag. Close-up of nurse, proud through tears, when she gets the news.

III. Student films, then the equivalent of our American Westerns. There I celebrated my greatest and most prolonged triumphs.

Young student, usually called Hans-Heinz or Horst-Juergen, scion of prominent, wealthy family, arrives at Heidelberg University, rents room—always overlooking the Nekar River—meets daughter (Elfriede or Jutta, lovely long blond curls) of landlady (impoverished kindly widow of heroic German officer who lies in eternal sleep in French soil). Romance begins, breath-taking outdoor shots, young couple boating on the Neckar, hiking, climbing vineyards, holding hands, and sipping wine at picturesque inn (comedy shot of someone at next table eating pig's knuckles and sauerkraut). They are joined by other student-landlady's-daughter combinations. Some jerk has brought a lute hung with gay ribbons, so they sing German student songs, linking arms and swaying in unison.

Hans-Heinz or Horst-Juergen is pledged into fraternity and proudly wears *couleur* ribbon and cap. Obnoxious student—unpleasantly drunk—stares at Elfriede-Jutta. A duel! Hans-Heinz-Horst-Juergen is wounded; prominent wealthy parents thus discover romance. Accuse landlady of trying to snag rich son-in-law. She proudly rejects young scion as suitor for her daughter. Young scion moves to other rented room, also overlooking Neckar. He's heartbroken (close-up of him: *not* smiling). Breath-taking scenic shot in which he saunters off all alone, boating, hiking, climbing vineyards, holding his own hands. Sipping wine at picturesque inn (Elfriede-Jutta's face appearing in wineglass), he decides life without those long blond curls not worth living. Leaves farewell note, goes to top of Heidelberg Castle, where he is spotted by kindly old professor who talks him out of jumping. Professor informs parents—stern father would rather have his son dead—but mother, having herself been daughter of impoverished heroic German officer's widow accepts Elfriede-Jutta. Final tableau of picturesque inn where they are joined by the creep with the lute. They sing "Gaudeamus igitur . . ."

This story I played in twenty-three variations and under twenty-three different titles. Sometimes I won the duel and that's the way the romance was discovered, sometimes I had a rival and I was the one who got drunk. Sometimes Elfriede-Jutta wanted to jump; but in every one of them we went boating, walked through vineyards, held hands, sang those student songs, and swayed in unison.

At that time I bought my first automobile. It was a tiny fire-engine-red convertible. Two people, if they were sufficiently fond of each other to endure a cuddling proximity, could ride in it. It involved complicated acrobatics to enter and leave that small bathtub on wheels. But it was my first car and I was terribly proud of it. It greatly enhanced my popularity and helped me to spread happiness to the opposite sex.

I christened the car "Nora" after my current greatest love.

Papa owned a huge Graef & Stift, the Austrian equivalent of the English Rolls-Royce. It sported a custom-made body with special headlights, fog lights, searchlights, a horn, siren, and klaxon, spare tires with chrome covers mounted on the front fenders, toolboxes and hydraulic jacks strapped to the running board, and a tremendous baggage rack with belts and buckles. It also had a double floor for smuggling his favorite cigars.

Under the dashboard was a panel which lit up with six different messages: Stop, Go, Slower, Faster, Home, and To the Opera. Papa never used that panel because he always sat in front next to our driver. Papa's seat, with comfortable armrests and special soft upholstery, had been widened, so it took up two thirds of the allotted space in front. That was the reason why we could only have narrow chauffeurs!

An elaborate arrangement of pockets and bags for road maps, cigars, cigar cutters, and cigar holders surrounded him, plus one rear and two side mirrors, so he could always see and communicate with Mama. Mama sat propped up in the left rear seat, her two Maltese terriers on her lap, covered by an automobile rug. How they ever managed to breathe I shall never know.

Mama had trouble with her sinuses, so when the car was driven with the top down, which Papa preferred, she wore a combination cap-goggles-face mask. How *she* ever managed to breathe I shall also never know.

Traveling in that car was no simple matter: dusters had to be worn, pillows taken along, footrests, armrests, blankets, and thermos bottles—all within easy reach. To change a tire was an hour's job and to put up the top took forty-five minutes. In sudden rain we were always drenched. Of course, neither

Papa nor Mama ever considered learning to drive a car; the chauffeur to whom they entrusted their lives was looked upon with the same awe and admiration that today we bestow upon a spaceman.

So when I telephoned Papa to tell him that I too had joined the ranks of the automobilists, his first question was: "Who recommended your chauffeur?"

"What chauffeur?" I laughed. "I am my own chauffeur, I took driving lessons and—"

Cavaradossi's scream of agony (Tosca, Act II) could be heard. If I had informed Papa that I was about to join a leper colony, he couldn't have been more upset.

"Ah—ai—oh—no—no, Elsa, come here quickly, the boy is driving a car, he will kill himself!" A suppressed sob of Mama's became audible.

"Walter, I implore you, listen to me." Papa's voice rose a full octave in pitch. "Driving a car is a job for a professional, like being a singer. Except that amateur singing is not dangerous. Amateur driving is *fatal.*"

He talked for twenty minutes until I reminded him that I had reversed charges and he was paying for that call. "Oh, my God, that too," he groaned, and hung up. Three hours later a telegram arrived:

BESEECH YOU NOT TO PLUNGE AGED PARENTS INTO MISERY.
YOUR UNHAPPY FATHER.

I should have listened to him.

Not that I plunged them into misery, but *I* went nearly broke and crazy with little Nora. She was a red lemon. Nothing worked. In the middle of Berlin's busiest intersection she would stall and I had to get out and push her. Her electrical system managed to get me nineteen traffic tickets for driving without lights. The salesman from whom I had purchased the car had left town and I learned that it had been an experimental model that had been discontinued after thirty-one cars were sold. Mine was the thirty-first.

One day while driving in the country I was surprised to see that a wheel was passing me on my left. With an unbelieving double-take I realized that it was MY wheel and four seconds later I was scraping along on the axle. I was on a lonely road and somehow the car caught fire. I watched it burn, praying all the while that nobody would come by and interrupt the kindly holocaust.

Nobody did—and the cremation was a complete one. My aged parents were happy; and I was happy, because the car was a total loss and I was fully insured.

Later on an astrologer told me that I unwisely had bought Nora on a day when Uranus conjuncted Mars and squared Jupiter. Which explained it all.

For one week I rode the subway. Then I bought a racing car that could do a hundred thirty-five miles an hour. This time I did not call Papa.

Become a movie star and see the world! That is one of the few glories of our profession. I went to Rome to play the lead in a film called *Addio, Giovinezza*. It was a most original story: Mario, young student, scion of wealthy family, arrives in Rome to enroll at university. Rents room overlooking river Tiber. Meets Gina (lovely long black curls) daughter of landlady. Boating on the river, climbing the seven hills of Rome, drinking Chianti at picturesque *taverna* (comedy shot of slob at next table eating spaghetti), etc., etc., etc.—on to happy end.

But I didn't care. Three wonderful months in the Eternal City. I bought an Alfa Romeo and fell passionately in love with a tall, lithe, sensuous creature called Carmela, who spoke only Italian.

I wish the Berlitz School would adopt her teaching methods.

She also doubled as an excellent Cicerone and took great pride in showing me the wonders of Rome: the Colosseum at moonlight, St. Peter's at sunrise, and the view from her apartment in the afternoon. But alas! There is a sad saying in show business: "We were terribly in love—but the show closed." The picture had come to an end. The farewell at the railway station was heartbreaking. We both sobbed out promises to write and vows to stay faithful; but I had to leave to start location shooting for my next film—in Heidelberg.

I came down with make-up poisoning and only the left side of my face could be photographed. My leading lady was furious about it because she was forced to play all our love scenes with her right profile—her bad side—to the camera.

After returning to Berlin, where we finished the film in the studio, my ailment turned into a full-fledged case of lead poisoning. Because I had signed a contract for another film in Paris, that picture had to be finished by a certain date. In the French picture I was to play neither a student nor a naval cadet, and was not even seduced by an alluring vamp. It was a story of a struggling young painter, and the script by Maurice Dekobra was really good. Besides, it was one of the first pictures made with sound.

I was in agony. It felt like lying in an anthill. Itching, crawling, prickling, creeping, stinging pains. Dermatology had a field day experimenting with me. All was tried on me—rays and lotions, salves and ointments.

So I could sleep at night my doctor prescribed heavy sedation: two big tablets of Luminal. One evening, being especially uncomfortable, I took three pills with a glass of water that stood next to my bed. What I *didn't* know was that my sweet idiot old housekeeper had already dissolved two tablets in that glass—"so the dear boy will get a good rest"—and of course had forgotten to tell me about it. The following morning she couldn't rouse me; she got frantic and called the producer of the film. He got frantic because that day three hundred fifty extras had been hired and he *needed* me. The studio doctor, with orders to bring me in dead or alive, learned about the Luminal, loaded me on a stretcher, took me to the studio and made me sniff cocaine. Within two minutes I was up—jolly, bright, and terribly talkative. I felt most intelligent. After about five hours the cocaine began to wear off, so Dr. Hoellenreich, for that was the monster's name, gave me some more. He kept that up for the next five days until my part was finished. He showed me the proper way to use the stuff: a little mound of that innocuous-looking white powder on the back of the hand, bring the hand up to your nose, two quick sniffs—and lick the hand so nothing goes to waste. As the days wore on the interval between sniffs became shorter. A few people warned me of the dangers of becoming an addict, but I felt too good and too light to listen. Dr. Hoellenreich personally brought me to the railway station to see me off to Paris and handed me a small box with dope to carry me over on my trip. He left me with the fatherly advice to gradually slow down on the stuff.

Shortly before the train arrived in Paris, two French nuns settled in my compartment and we fell into a conversation. In my talkativeness I told them that I used cocaine—on doctor's orders—and related the whole story. They suggested that I go to a hospital to get my skin and my system cleansed and call off the silly film: "Why don't you take one big sniff now," one of them suggested, "and then throw the rest of the stuff out of the window."

I still don't know why, but that's what I did. They said they would pray for me.

Their prayers must have been very powerful, for when the train pulled into the Gare St. Lazare, there stood the producer of the film to tell me that shooting had to be postponed for two weeks and that he hoped I wouldn't mind. I didn't and took a taxi to the hospital where the good sisters worked.

Sister Célestine and Sister Marie-Louise—wherever you are—thank you.

Her name was Arlette and she smelled of Houbigant's Quelques Fleurs.

She was terribly, terribly chic: limbs slim and endlessly long, eyes the color of deep chartreuse, hair of flaming amber, hands narrow and fragile, cheekbones high, complexion of pale porcelain. The voice low and melodious. I was in awe of her delicate beauty, but she ate like a horse. On our first dinner date she suggested that I take her to Hôtel Rond Point de Champs Elysées, whose restaurant was very famous. Arlette looked like a cover of *Vogue* and all eyes followed her when we were shown to our table. I felt proud.

I was handed what I thought was an exquisitely bound first edition. But it turned out to be the bill of fare. Rich, varied, elaborate, and elegant.

In fact, it was so elegant that the prices were not even mentioned.

The maître d'hôtel stepped up, his manner endearing and benevolent. He took the menu away from me, as if to say: "We won't need this, will we?" He winked at me. I didn't like it.

"Madame is open to suggestions?"

Madame lifted her finely chiseled chin and looked ahead . . . She was!

"Caviar Mollosol?" He sounded a little apprehensive.

She lowered her long eyelashes in agreement and inclined her head gently toward me, thus forcing me into silent acknowledgment.

"Potée bourguignonne?"

"*Charmant.*" She smiled.

"*Langouste, grillée, à la crème?*"

She touched my hand. "You'll *like* that."

"*Faisan sous cloche, ris sauvage?*"

Down came the eyelids.

"*Petit filet en croustade, asperges à la sauce Molière?*"

She glanced him a small thank you as if he had just lit her cigarette.

He had gained confidence: "*Les crêpes flambées au Kirsch!*"

It sounded like a command.

"*Fromages variés!*

"*Café diable!*

"*Des petits riens . . .*" The last was said condescendingly.

"*Ahmm—les petits riens,*" she purred (they turned out to be candies).

The maître d' flashed his teeth at me and with a casual "*Merci, monsieur*" he was irretrievably gone. But in the place where he stood appeared the sommelier, smiling, jolly, holding —but not parting with—the wine list. Madame was not only open to suggestions, she was eager! Waiters are quick to recognize a pigeon when they see one; so before he was through ordering wine for us, practically everyone in the place was swarming around our table, setting dishes, silverware, and glasses. An atmosphere of general rejoicing could definitely be felt.

Way back, when *langouste grillée à la crème* had first been suggested, there had arisen in me a slight suspicion that I might not have enough money on me to pay for the feast. By the time the sommelier had descended into the cellar to search for the rare vintages he felt we should sample, that suspicion had ballooned into a horrible certainty. Now I KNEW that a swift current of adversity was swirling me further and further up the good creek—and no paddle in sight.

There is an old saying, "When rape is inevitable—you might as well relax and enjoy it." I found it small comfort.

Arlette was a lovely companion. Being nearsighted, she brought her face with those luminous amber eyes and that low voice quite close to mine. It was like having a conversation with an owl.

A large bubble of anxiety was growing larger and larger in my stomach. I couldn't eat much. But there was nothing wrong with *her* feeding habits. With the steady, resolute rhythm of a Channel swimmer's strokes, her slender arms and fragile hands traveled from plate to mouth. She ate for both of us.

I lingered over my brandy and kept on lingering, until the solicitude of the headwaiter, inquiring again and again if there wouldn't be anything else we wanted, shamed me into asking for the bill.

It came to about five times the amount I had dreaded. With great nonchalance I got up and sauntered to the telephone in the hotel lobby.

I called the Pathé Film Company and talked to the night watchman.

I called my producer and talked to his cook.

I called my director and talked to his mother-in-law. It was a Saturday and everybody I knew was out. I even thought of calling Papa in Vienna, but somehow it didn't seem practical.

So I simply walked over to the room clerk and registered as a hotel guest. Only the presidential suite was vacant. I mumbled something about having my luggage sent over "*bientôt*" and tipped him all the cash I carried. I walked back to the restaurant, signed the check, and had it charged to Apartment 9.

Then I told it all to Arlette.

She laughed and found it "*très chic.*"

I invited her up for a nightcap, but she was a woman of principle: "Not on our first date," she laughed, and hailed a cab.

But on Sunday afternoon she visited me—for a tea and "*amuse bouche.*"

I found that "*très chic.*"

Monday morning Pathé Film Company bailed me out.

A few days after I returned to Berlin, my telephone rang. It was Willy F., a well-known fellow leading man.

"Walter, you rascal, you old reprobate, you sneaky Don Juan," he began, "you certainly do get around! I hear you had quite a romance with Hanne P.!"

Hanne was one of the secretaries of our big boss at UFA. She was very attractive, great fun, and she got around quite a lot. Being a cavalier of the old Viennese school, I denied any intimacy. But Willy pressed on:

"Why, you great big liar—you don't have to play coy with me—she told me so herself."

"Then the lady was bragging," was my noble reply.

The more he kept insinuating, searching, probing with rib-poking man-to-man talk, the nobler I got.

The whole conversation didn't make sense. I couldn't figure out what he was after.

The following morning another, somewhat older actor, George A. who had quite a reputation as a lady-killer, called. Again about Hanne and me. The same pitch!

Now I was really puzzled. I took Hanne to lunch and quizzed her: that gay little charmer, it turned out, was in the family way and had chosen BOTH Willy and George as heads of that family. (German law recognizes dual paternity, with all its financial responsibilities. But if a *third* individual can be found who admits to have enjoyed her favors at the same crucial period, then the lady doesn't have a legal leg to stand on.)

My puzzlement was over: the two dear boys were frantically looking for a THIRD. Happily they did not find one.

The great Oskar Straus, of *Waltz Dream* and *The Chocolate Soldier* fame wanted me for his new operetta *Hochzeit in Hollywood* in Vienna. It was a big success and I played it for two hundred performances at the old Johann Strauss Theater. I stayed on for Franz Lehar's *Friederike*. Meister Lehar personally conducted the first hundred performances, only because he so dearly loved to take curtain calls. At the end of the show, the moment the last chord had faded, he dropped the baton and ran like a weasel through the crowded orchestra pit, nimbly sprinting over musicians' feet, dodging violins, trombones, and protruding bass drums. Up the stairs he leaped, three steps at a time, and landed breathless in the wings. He stretched out his hand and whispered: "Pull me out!" With physical resistance and great reluctance he allowed himself to be dragged on-stage. There he stood, in helpless wonder, over-awed and moved by the slowly growing realization that all that applause was meant for him. One night, for fun, we made him wait—we ignored his outstretched hand and his whispers. But he didn't wait long; unassisted, he catapulted on, pretending that he had been shoved and waving a "naughty, naughty" finger at some imaginary person in the wings.

At home things were not good. Poor Papa was going through a severe crisis with his voice. His nervousness before a performance had become pathological and he and Mama suffered agony every time he had to sing.

Only once before had he had trouble with his voice. He was then a very young man. Gustav Mahler had just brought him to the Vienna Opera. Overnight a hoarse quality had appeared when he sang; the instrument that had responded with such natural ease became suddenly strained and harsh. A thorough examination brought forth the verdict every singer dreads most: nodes on the vocal cords.

Professor Epstein, the famous laryngologist, operated. "You are NOT to use your voice after the operation," he warned. "No singing, NO TALKING, not even *whispering*. You must give the cords a complete rest and a chance to heal." And with brutal frankness he said: "Only after three months of absolute silence will you know if you still have your voice. It's a fifty-fifty chance."

Then began the hardest period of his young life. What if his voice were gone? What would he do then? He had only attended school until he was fourteen years old; the only training he ever had was as a blacksmith. And now he was married, he had a child, and the second was on the way. After the operation he and Mama traveled to Italy, where they lived in complete isolation and very cheaply in a small village. They knew nobody and there was no temptation to talk. With Mama he communicated only by writing. His landlord believed him to be a mute. Daily they went on long walks, but on one of these walks Mama tripped, stumbled, and fell headlong into a small ravine that ran next to the path. Papa screamed: *"Elsa, um Gottes Willen."* She was then heavy with child; with me to be specific. The fall didn't do any damage, not to her and, as far as I know, not to me, although it does give me a lovely alibi whenever I goof or mess up things. But now their agony was doubled by the fear that Papa's scream may have torn open the healing cord.

On the ninety-third day after the operation they went to Mass at the village church. Then they returned home and Papa began to try out his voice. Very softly at first, then increasing the volume, carefully and gradually, testing the instrument until he felt confident and opened up wide and to full range. Papa often told me that never, never would he forget the expression on Mama's face when he began to sing. The transition from numb fear, to hope, to relief, and to the unspeakable happiness when she realized that the voice was back in all its rich, glorious, full beauty.

"We cried and laughed and shouted thanks; I sang and sang, until all the neighbors came to see what was going on and the whole morning exploded into a wonderful fiesta."

But now the situation was different; he was fifty-five years old and very much aware that the life of a singer is a short one. The panic of the closing door was upon him. He had developed a fear of high notes. The knowledge that he would have to sing a high C or even a B flat was enough to make him cancel the performance, he transposed wherever he could, but every time he walked out on the stage it was an ordeal.

About a year later he was singing a concert in Berlin. I was then rehearsing a play by Wedekind. The stage-door man called me aside. "Call your father right away—it's urgent."

I ran to the next phone. "Come over as soon as possible!" Mama sounded excited. Ten minutes later I entered the Hotel Adlon. Papa stood in the middle of the room. "Sit down at the piano—play C major!" He sang an arpeggio. I rose on the scale, increasing each chord by half a note. The voice sounded excellent. I grew apprehensive when he reached A, but he continued without a trace of nervousness. Then B flat—easy, free, no strain; B natural—a glorious tone, young, rich, powerful—I couldn't believe my ears, didn't think it possible. And then his voice soared on, effortless, majestically, like a shimmering ball of gold up to a magnificent radiant high C.

I was so choked up I couldn't talk. "Thank God," Papa said softly, "there is nothing wrong with my voice, my career is NOT over, I can still stay on top, I am not yet ready for the sausage machine!"

This is what had happened. After that concert a man came into his dressing room. "Herr Kammersaenger, I know that you are a very worried man. You are afraid! Let me assure you that you are not losing your voice, you only lost your way. Please give me an hour of your time. Here is my phone number." And he left. The card read: "Prf. Flamm singing teacher."

Singing teachers are a special breed of people. To become one, you only have to say: "I am a singing teacher!" That's your diploma, these are your credentials. To supervise your four- and five-year-olds playing with blocks in the kindergarten, to teach them the A B C, to treat the corns on your feet, to cut your hair, give you a massage—all require proof of training—and a license. But that rarest gift of God, that wonderful intangible, the human voice? Anybody can fool around with it; every broken-down, third-rate singer, every unsuccessful piano teacher, every flunked-out music student. All you need is a room with a piano, photos of a few well-known singers on the wall (the implication being that they are "pupils"), and you are in business and automatically addressed as "Professor."

No mother ever looked into her newborn's crib and said with hopeful pride: "Someday this child will be a great singing teacher." (Or a great prompter in opera!) There are no schools to train the teachers of the human voice. That profession is usually the backwash and last resort of failure or old age.

To be, or to have been, a great singer is by no means a guarantee that one will be a good teacher. One of Papa's great fears throughout his life had always been the prospect that he might lose his money and be forced to earn his living teaching, because he felt completely incapable of passing on to others what HE could do so well.

Of course there are many wonderful exceptions: George

Bernard Shaw's dictum "Those who can . . . do! Those who can't . . . teach!" is not always correct. My father's early mentor, Adolf Robinson, was a great singer in his time and an equally great teacher. So were Jean de Reszke, Lilli Lehmann, Mme. Schoen-Renée, Vera Schwarz, Stella Eisner-Ames, Garcia, and many, many others. However, there is one thing ALL singing teachers have in common, the good ones *and* the charlatans: whenever an established artist finds himself in trouble vocally and turns to one of them for help (as he would to a doctor or a psychiatrist) they gleefully inform all and everybody: "Poor X.Y. hasn't a tone left in his throat; has lost his voice completely—now he comes to me and wants me to save it! I will have to change the placement of his voice, he will have to forget everything he ever learned, it will take years!"

These pronouncements are eagerly repeated in the flourishing gossip mills of the music world and can be very damaging to a career, as the slightest indisposition is immediately taken as unmistakable proof that the end has come. So Papa shied away from that tribe and avoided them like the plague. But what Flamm had said sounded so logical and hopeful that Papa invited him over. They talked for an hour and like a good physiotherapist he was able to remove the fear that had contracted his muscles, gave him courage, and restored his confidence.

They remained warm friends.

When Oskar Karlweiss, that wonderful actor and light comedian, left the show *Meine Schwester und ich,* I took over for him. It was a charming play with music and we played it all through the summer of 1930.

On Sunday morning, July 6, I left my apartment to go to the beach. After I closed the front door, I heard the telephone ring. I have always had a compulsion about answering phones, so I returned. "Mr. Slezak, I am speaking for Mr. Shubert from New York." The voice sounded as if someone decided to disguise it by pinching his nostrils together. "Mr. Shubert saw your play last night. He wants to engage you to come to America."

I immediately smelled a rat; a few weeks earlier, I had played a trick on a fellow actor, George Richter, retaliating for a whole chain of pranks. I asked an American girl friend who spoke German with a strong accent to call George and tell him that Mr. Carl Laemmle of Universal Pictures was in town, had seen him in his latest film, and was terribly impressed. Mr. Laemmle, she explained, felt that Mr. Richter possessed that rare, indefinable quality of stardom and he intended to bring him to Hollywood to launch him as "The Blond Valentino." Mr. Laemmle would like Mr. Richter to come and visit him at the Hotel Adlon, at 8 P.M. George immediately dyed his hair a light yellow. At the hotel he was told that Mr. Laemmle was out for the evening; so he sat and waited in the lobby, well past midnight, until the diminutive Mr. Laemmle walked in with his entourage. George stepped up to him and said with easy charm: "Here I *am*—your BLOND VALENTINO!" Mr. Laemmle looked up and said: "Get out of my way!"

I was amused that George should think me so naïve and fall for such a corny comeback, so I told the voice on the phone that I did not care to travel to America at this time, as I had firm commitments for the next six years, and FURTHERMORE I was certainly NOT interested in working for such a small and unimportant outfit as the Shuberts.

Well pleased with myself, I hung up and left the house to pick up Natasha, my current playmate, to go to the beach. Around noon, as we were sunning ourselves on a float, I mentioned the phone call. "But a Mr. Shubert from America IS in Berlin," she said. "I read it in the papers."

Then it hit me in a flash that many years earlier a fortune-teller had prophesied that I would go to live "across the big water and there find my luck and fortune."

"Oh, my God," I groaned, swam back to shore and began calling the big hotels. On my third try, the Hotel Adlon, a Mr. Shubert from New York *was* registered. They rang his suite, and the voice with the pinched nostrils answered. I stammered apologies, mumbled something about having believed that it was a joke, then raced back to town and walked in on Mr. J. J. Shubert, the theater magnate, who stood in the middle of the room, wearing a hat.

"How well do you speak English?" he asked.

I started to tell him the story of my life, how I had been in America as a child. "That'll do," he said, cutting me short. "Do you want to play the part I saw you in last night on Broadway?"

"Yes, please," I said, and bowed.

"O.K. . . . then I'll buy the play!"

Five minutes later the deal was closed, the contracts signed, and I was back in the street, dazed and bewildered. I called my parents, who were taking the waters in Marienbad: "Now we have lost the boy," I heard Mama cry on the other end of the phone.

Then began a round of farewell parties that lasted for eighty-six days. For an actor to be engaged to go to America was a big thing in 1930, and I accepted the admiration and envy that went with it with modest grace. Seventeen people—all important wheels in Berlin—gave me letters of introduction to important wheels in New York. Papa fitted me out with new luggage—heavy steamer trunks that weighed seventy-five pounds empty; Mama bought me sweaters and socks; and I read eight different books on LIFE IN AMERICA.

I went home to Tegernsee, but after two heartbreaking days of saying farewell, I got a wire from the Shubert office saying that I shouldn't leave until August 3. On August 1 the farewells began again, and again my trip was postponed to September 5, and then to September 19, and finally to October 1. By then, all the grief of parting had been spent, and Papa said, "I really hope you leave this time. I couldn't bear any more farewells." So I went back to Berlin and was accompanied by several friends to Hamburg from where my ship sailed—for a big, final blowout. Next morning I barely made it and had the biggest hangover of my life. When the S.S. *Milwaukee* pulled out to sea, I didn't know that I was leaving for good and that I would find my luck and fortune in America.

I did not know then that Mr. J. J. Shubert had given me much more than a chance to play on Broadway. If it weren't for him, I most probably would be fertilizer on some battlefield in France or in Russia, or occupying a traitor's grave for disobeying orders or expressing opinions.

My eternal gratitude goes to him.

During the trip I was seated at the captain's table.

"What's so precious about you anyway?" he asked during the first meal. I didn't understand what he meant. "Why should I worry about *you?*" He smiled and handed me a letter. I recognized the old woman's scribble of my grandmother: "Dear Herr Kapitaen, my grandson is sailing on your ship to America. Please keep an eye on him and drive carefully. Thank you—Antonia Wertheim, grandmother of Walter Slezak." So for the rest of the trip he kept sending me little messages: "Don't play the horses. I am watching you!" One night I was playing cards at three-thirty in the morning when his steward came over. "Captain says it's time to turn in."

During a heavy sea, when the dishes and crystal kept crashing off the tables, I got a note: "I AM driving carefully." He was a jovial old sea dog, but lost his humor completely at the captain's dinner when a young lady came in wearing nothing but an American flag wrapped about her. "Go to your cabin and take that off," he thundered. And when one of the guests presented him with a blue ribbon for the slowest ocean crossing, he got up and left the table.

On my first day in New York, I plunged into the gaudy carnival atmosphere of Times Square and Forty-second Street. I gaped at the lights, the Times Building, the electrical shoeshine parlors, the burlesque houses, and penny arcades. When I saw a bill of fare in a restaurant window and discovered that oysters were only forty-five cents a dozen (in Europe they are a great delicacy and are very small and very expensive), I walked in and ordered three dozen. The waitress looked surprised, but not as surprised as I when she brought them and I saw their size. I managed to eat only thirty-four.

Rehearsals had been set back again, until the middle of November, and I had time on my hands.

I took my seventeen letters of introduction and called the first important wheel, a banker on Wall Street. I was immediately ushered into his office. He was terribly nice. We chatted a few minutes about our mutual friends, and then he said: "All right, Mr. Slezak, what can I do for you?" That stumped me completely. I laughed and said: "Nothing, really." He laughed right back at me and said: "Whenever there is something I can do for you, do not fail to call on me." We shook hands, and I left. Then I tore up the sixteen other letters and resolved to meet poeple on my own.

I spent the next four weeks exploring that fabulous city and perfecting my English. I set myself a daily program of sight-seeing: the waterfront, where all the big luxury liners arrive and sail, the produce markets downtown on the West Side, the aquarium, then at the Battery, the fish markets on the East Side, Wall Street and Chinatown, Delancey Street and the Lower East Side with its kosher restaurants and Yiddish theaters, the Armenian section, the garment district and the flower markets, Yorkville and Harlem, where I discovered a synagogue whose entire congregation was colored and where the Jewish songs had an African beat. Everywhere I took my time, observed, tried to get into conversations, and had a meal.

I became an expert on the New York subway system—and, of course, on the cuisine of the various nationalities. It was then that I started my collection of recipes. When I was especially intrigued with a dish and they wouldn't give me the recipe, I analyzed it and tried it out at home.

My afternoons were spent in the movie houses, often seeing the same film several times, to study audience reaction and actor's timing. Every night I went to the theater, and I was surprised to find out that in America actors have to pay the full box-office price—the same as everybody else. In Europe one always got the courtesy of the house or sometimes "*Steuerkarten,*" where you paid just the tax on the ticket.

The first friend from Vienna I ran into was Erica Morini, the famous violinist. One Sunday night she took me along to a dinner party at "Aunt Jennie's."

Aunt Jennie was the largest, nicest, warmest, most vivacious, bell-shaped sixty-seven-year-old matriarch I have ever met—with a heart as big as Mount Whitney and a gregarious appetite and affection for people. Sunday dinner at her house was an institution—her son, grandchildren, scores of nephews and nieces and their spouses flocked there. Everybody brought someone along; it was always a seated dinner, generally for twenty-four. Through twenty-eight years of true friendship, until she left us at the age of ninety-five, she and her home became "my American family"—she accepted me BEFORE I had been a success on Broadway. When I was between shows, she often called and asked: "Walter, are you broke? Need any money?" To go out with her, to take her to dinner or to a show, was a real pleasure. She enjoyed EVERYTHING, and *said* so; and after you brought her back home, she left you with the feeling that you had entertained her royally. She was Aunt Jennie to everybody, except to her butler, Anton. To him she was Mrs. J. W. Schiffer.

Anton was the perfect butler to end all perfect butlers. He was elegance and dignity personified. The first time I walked into the house, he inclined his head slightly in greeting and intoned: "Permit me to welcome you to Mrs. Schiffer's home." Then he opened the doors to the salon with a flourish and announced me; CORRECTLY pronouncing my name. While serving dinner, he was completely stone-faced, never laughed or smiled in reaction to anything funny that was said at the table. Try as I might, I was NEVER able to break him up.

One Sunday afternoon, I had a wonderful time entertaining a young lady and felt that going to Aunt Jennie's for dinner might be an anticlimax. So, I telephoned her that I was sick. "Walter," she commanded, "you go right to bed." I obeyed, and we ordered food from room service. Half an hour later there was a knock on the door of my sitting room. I yelled: "Come in!" thinking it was the waiter with our dinner. But with a cheery "A very good evening to you, sir," Anton walked into the bedroom and said: "Frightfully sorry, I am in the wrong apartment," turned on his heel, and was gone, but not without leaving behind the most elaborate arrangement of nests of hot food containers, filled with chicken, broth, and lots of other nourishing goodies. To Aunt Jennie he reported he had found me in bed but altogether not too uncomfortable.

The next time he greeted me at the door of the mansion, there was just the slightest glint of roguish appreciation in his eye, as if he wanted to say: "I perfectly understand, sir."

A few years later—I was then living in the country and had an early Monday appointment—I stayed over at Aunt Jennie's in one of the many guest rooms.

At eight in the morning the door opened ever so gently and Anton's mellow voice crept through the dense fog of my sleep. "Good morning, sir! Mrs. Schiffer asked me to inquire how you've slept."

I rasped: "Fine," turned over, and heard his exit line: "Mrs. Schiffer will be pleased!"

At the dawn of day I want to be alone. I want to wake up and rise, unassisted, in silence and on my own terms.

Seconds later Anton was back. "Mrs. Schiffer would like to know if you are a *Times* or *Tribune* reader." With my eyes still closed I mumbled, "BOTH," and tried to shut out the world for a few more precious minutes. But Anton was back, bearing the morning papers on a silver tray like the head Jokanaan. "And what would you desire for breakfast, sir?"

"Oh, anything," I groaned.

"White toast—or whole wheat?"

"I don't care!" He went to order my breakfast and returned.

"May I draw your bath, sir?"

"Oh no—thank you—I'll . . . I'll do it myself."

"May I lay out your clothes, sir?" he asked, pointing to the heap of haberdashery that lay on the floor, covering my blue suit, where I had stepped out of it the night before.

I was close to tears. "Anton, PLEASE—" I begged. "Don't play games with me—it's too early . . . leave me alone—go away."

"Very good, sir," he said, smiling pleasantly.

Later he reported to Mrs. Schiffer that Mr. Slezak was a gentleman who cherished solitude in the morning.

Rehearsals for *Meet My Sister* finally got under way. It was a strange experience for me to work in English—the fourth language in which I had acted—the lingo of the theater was new and many of the changes that were made to Americanize the play didn't make sense to me.

After we were rehearsing for about two weeks, a small

dark gentleman walked into the theater, pointed at me, and asked: "Who is that man?"

Our director rushed to the footlights. "Why, that's Mr. Slezak, the star from Germany." And he introduced me to Mr. *Lee* Shubert, J.J.'s brother.

"You didn't play that role in Berlin," he said accusingly. "It was another man, much shorter and a little older." All eyes slowly turned to me: first squinting with suspicion, then opening wide with unconcealed abhorrence. Everybody backed away from me. I sensed danger and my brain worked hard and fast. "When did you see the show in Berlin, Mr. Shubert?" I asked very casually. "In March," he replied, with frost on his face. "Oh, that's too bad," I laughed, slightly forced. "During March, I was out of the show with appendicitis. You must have seen my understudy, Oskar Karlweiss."

"Oh? Yes, that's possible," said Mr. Lee, mollified, and added, "He was very good!" He left the stage. The incident was closed. The looks of abhorrence turned into smiles, and I was no longer a pariah.

What had happened was this: Mr. Lee, on his yearly trip to Europe, had seen and liked the show, but as it was a musical—the exclusive domain of his brother J.J.—he suggested, *via inter-office memo,* because the brothers never talked to each other, that J.J. have a look at the play on HIS yearly trip to Europe. And Mr. J.J.—PRAISE THE LORD—had come in July and seen me. I was lucky.

We played *Meet My Sister* for a short tryout week at the Majestic Theatre in Brooklyn. In the excitement and the turmoil of the opening and in my wondrous realization that I had just given my first performance in ENGLISH . . . I had completely forgotten that it was Christmas Eve. All my colleagues rushed home to their families, and I found myself alone on the sidewalk of Flatbush Avenue. I took a subway to New York and went to a speak-easy. There I sat over a glass of lousy beer, crying with loneliness, feeling homesick and terribly sorry for myself. But the following morning, the Brooklyn *Daily Eagle* soothed me with a good write-up and after the New York opening on New Year's Eve, when I read that I was a matinee idol (that term had to be explained to me) and was called "The German Chevalier," who exuded charm to a remarkable degree, I was again on top of the world and called Papa in Vienna.

On a local call, Papa would think nothing of talking for an hour, but the moment he heard the words "LONG DISTANCE" he became excited, took out his watch, and talked very fast and very loud, interrupting ever so often to announce: "Two more minutes, a minute and a half, only forty seconds left . . . fifteen seconds," and then he hung up in the middle of a sentence.

His sense of economy regarded it as a major crime to talk longer than three minutes. Of course, at first, we said all the idiotic things, told each other what time it was and asked about the weather, but when I began quoting my write-ups, he suddenly yelled: "Mail them. Good-by."

Dying is the same all over the world; only the ceremonies preceding the final disposing of the body vary in many countries.

Shortly after I arrived in America, I received the sad news that my dentist had died—"passed away" was the phrase used—and that the funeral services would be held at Koke's Funeral Parlor, on West Seventy-ninth Street.

In dark suit with black tie, I walked along Seventy-ninth Street, looking for the address—and nearly bumped into a huge, uniformed doorman who stood in the street, joking and laughing with a taxi driver. I asked him where I might find Koke's Funeral Parlor. Immediately, his mien changed from hilarity to deep sorrow and sympathy, and he informed me that I was standing right in front of it.

He took me gently by the arm and led me carefully to an elevator. "Whose funeral, please?" he asked with infinite tenderness. "Dr. Van Wehlen." "Second floor." I stepped into the elevator, and organ music came out of a loud-speaker. That startled me. When I got out at the second floor, I was ushered into a long, somber room. At first I thought it was a concert hall. Wall brackets with orange-colored light bulbs that were twisted into a flamelike shape dimly illuminated the cheap Gobelin imitations on the walls and there were rows of chairs. At the far end a stage—and on that stage stood a casket.

Before I had a chance to sit down, a young man walked up to me. He wore a cutaway, also gray gloves whose ends were rolled back and left exposed a strip of pink flesh between cuff and glove. That was the only bright thing about him. He pointed toward the stage.

"Will you please view the body?"

"No, thank you"—I hedged—"don't think I—"

"Will you PLEASE view the body—" he repeated with quiet authority.

"Yes, sir, I will," replied I, obedient little thing that I am. I walked up to the casket. The lower part was closed and the upper part open, like a cigar box. On the rim of the part that was open there was attached a light fixture with a little pull chain—the kind one finds on pianos and music stands. The electric light bulb was pink and shone a ghastly light on the face of the dear departed doctor.

When alive, he had many outstanding attributes, but physical beauty was never one of them. The undertakers evidently were aware of that and had tried to improve his looks. They adorned him with rosy cheeks, rosy lips, carefully penciled eyebrows, and managed to produce a smile on his face. It was so sad—he looked indecent, like an old playgirl on a frilled bed.

I quickly said a little prayer and sat down. The place was filling up with mourners, all properly solemn, except for one couple who sat in front of me. They had the giggles; and the more they tried to control themselves, the more hysterical they became.

Everybody waited. Then a man in shirt sleeves stuck his head into the door, pointed to his wrist watch, and impatiently ordered the young man with the gray gloves to get the show rolling. Whereupon he, with one simultaneous movement, adjusted his tie with one hand and checked his fly with the other. Satisfied that everything was *comme il faut,* he walked toward the stage—erect, strong, and with well-controlled grief—placed himself in front of the casket, faced the audience, and executed a deep, reverent bow in the direction of the poor widow.

I settled back because I expected him to sing, but he didn't. Instead he repeated his bowing until it looked like a penguin ceremony. The poor widow didn't get whatever it was he wanted to convey to her—so he took recourse to broad pantomime. Like an aerial artist in the circus will show that he will now do a triple somersault from the high wire—and be caught by his partner in mid-air, all without the benefit of a net—so he demonstrated that he was about to close the casket and that she should say farewell. The poor little soul understood, walked up, kissed the dear doctor good-by, and was escorted back to her seat. The young man pulled the chain of the electric light fixture; the light went out, he unscrewed it from the casket and attached it to a music stand nearby. Then he closed the open part of the casket, locked it with a key, and handed the key to the widow, who looked very bewildered.

All this was done with agonizing slowness. In measured steps he walked to the side of the stage where stood a large vase with artificial lilies. He carried them, one lily at a time, to the casket and laid them down—each one with a tender farewell gesture. Every eye in the room followed him—like a slow-motion tennis match.

After that was accomplished, he placed the music stand center stage and pulled the little chain. The pink light came up again and he bowed toward the door. Every eye followed him. At the door a gentleman was waiting in a dark suit, leafing through his notes. He caught the signal from the stage, adjusted his necktie, but refrained from checking his fly. There was nothing insecure about *him.*

He was the rabbi, and as he walked up the aisle, he intoned the prayers for the dead in Hebrew. Four women, scattered throughout the audience, began shrill wailings. When the rabbi spoke English, they were quiet. Every time he slipped in a Hebrew word, up came their wailing. (I later learned that they were professional mourners hired for the occasion and that the degree of their wailing bore a certain relationship to the financial arrangements that had been made with them.)

The rabbi's speech was, as my trained actor's ear soon discovered, one he had delivered many times before. It was like the six hundredth performance of a play, where nobody on stage bothers to think what the play is about or what the scene means. The mouth talks the dialogue and the brain thinks of something else—usually counts the house.

Just then a lady tiptoed in. I moved over to make room for her, and she sat down next to me. She stretched her neck, looked around and cased the joint, then produced a small handkerchief, dabbed her nose with it, and started sniveling. She pointed to the casket, nudged me, whispering:

"Isn't it awful—such a darling."

I agreed.

"So many bastards are alive—and he"—she blew her nose —"such a darling."

"And SO young," she continued.

The dear doctor was sixty-nine, which, of course, is too young to die—but not SO young. But politely I nodded in agreement.

"And now our beloved Dr. Van Wehlen passed away and his soul has been received"—the rabbi droned on.

The lady suddenly looked at me, full of suspicion, excused herself, walked over to the man with gray gloves, and asked him something. He smiled, shook his head, and pointed to the floor above. She smiled back, thanked him graciously, and hurried out.

It then dawned on me that the dear woman had been crying at the wrong funeral. The one she wanted to attend was on the third floor.

Then and there I made up my mind that if I should die in America, which is most likely, I want to be buried by Western Union.

I am full of faults, one of them being that I never listen to the names of people I am being introduced to; so one evening after a large dinner party at Aunt Jennie's, I found myself playing backgammon with a small, birdlike gentleman. He got up in the middle of the game and said: "You play terribly."

I was a little offended and said: "Well I am NOT a *professional.*"

"Neither am I," he replied.

"What *do* you do?" I asked. He looked at me surprised: "I am a composer! What do YOU do?"

"I am an actor!"

"Are you a good actor?"

"I most certainly am! Are you a good composer?"

He looked even more surprised, shrugged his shoulders, and said: "People seem to think so. I am Jerome Kern!" We began to talk, and he told me that he had not seen me in *Meet My Sister* (which had since closed), and talked about a musical he was then writing, *Music in the Air,* and asked if I would sing for him. I said yes, but only on a stage, where I have the protection of the footlights. Nothing terrifies me more than to have to get up in a room and perform.

Two days later, he met me in the Old Globe Theatre. I had brought an accompanist and was trembling with fear. Mrs. Kern was there, and Oscar Hammerstein and Mrs. Hammerstein. I began with a little song I had sung in *Meet My Sister*. After about twenty bars, Mr. Kern said, "That's all!" put on his coat, and walked out. I was furious at his rudeness and started putting away my music, when Mr. Hammerstein called up: "WE would like to hear more." So I fought down my anger and humiliation, did my "whole repertory," and went home. About a week later Aunt Jennie called: "Walter, I am so glad. I hear you got the job." At first, I didn't know what she was talking about.

"Jerry Kern wants you for his next musical," she explained, full of impatience. I called him at his home.

"We'll start rehearsing in September," he said, very matter of fact. "Flo Ziegfeld, who is producing, will get in touch with you about the contract."

"But I thought you didn't like me," I complained. "You walked out during my first song!"

"I had heard enough—why should I prolong the agony of auditioning?"

I was never able to find out if he meant MY agony or HIS agony.

Until I became an American citizen in 1937, I always fell victim to the six-month-layoff clause. That is a ruling of Actors Equity that prevents an alien from accepting a job in the theater for six months following the closing of his last show. He also is barred from working in summer stock. That clause is mainly directed against our English cousins, preventing their influx, and thus protecting the employment of U.S.

actors. To me it was very harmful, because it took the impetus out of my career.

So in 1932 I returned to Europe and made a film. One day I picked up a paper and read that Flo Ziegfeld had died. I wrote to Jerome Kern but never got an answer, so I figured the whole deal was off and signed with Gebrueder Rotter, the poor man's counterpart to the Shuberts, to play in the new Oscar Straus operetta *Eine Frau die weiss was sie will,* with the great Fritzi Massary.

Three days after we had begun to rehearse, I received a letter from Jerome Kern's lawyer, explaining that they had another producer, a former showgirl named Peggy Fears, now the wife of A. C. Blumenthal, who used to be one of Ziegfeld's backers; and that they were expecting me on October 15.

I booked passage and called at the American consulate to get another visitor's permit. The consul asked me if I wouldn't prefer to take an emigration visa in case I wanted to become an American citizen. I thought it was a nice idea, and he casually handed me what six months later was to become a most priceless commodity.

Beg as I would, the brothers Rotter wouldn't release me from my contract unless I paid them an exorbitant sum of money that bore no relation to my salary. Fritzi Massary, our star, had been informed that I wanted to leave the show, and I overheard her saying, "I am tired. I refuse to rehearse with another man. After all, Slezak has a contract. Why don't you take away his passport? Then he won't be able to leave." Four hours later I was crossing the border into France and took the boat from Cherbourg to New York. It was the only time in my life that I had run out on a contract, but it was just as well, as a few months later the Nazi madness broke out, the show was closed, Fritzi Massary couldn't work any more, the Rotters fled the country, and Oscar Straus emigrated to America.

Music in the Air was the happiest show I ever did. Wonderful music, an excellent book, and two great artists like Kern and Hammerstein to work with. Reinald Werrenrath, Natalie Hall, Tullio Carminati—all were such nice colleagues—and the GIRLS, never before or after have I seen so many gorgeous females assembled on one stage—we had inherited from Flo Ziegfeld twelve of his loveliest long-stemmed beauties. They weren't overly bright, but, oh, what bodies and what perfectly symmetrical faces, devoid of any expression but a fixed smile. We also had sixteen singers. Not only did they possess first-class voices, but they too were lookers. And, last but not least, a group of ten tiny dancers, who doubled playing children—but they sure weren't. I was then thirty years old, and I suffered all the joys and pangs of indecision an eager gourmet might feel at a smörgåsbord.

Just to be on the safe side, I invented a "wife," Olga, who was living in Vienna and was expected to join me in New York presently. "Oh, if it weren't for Olga!" became my battle cry, my moat, and my drawbridge.

In 1933, when *Music in the Air* closed, I was again hit by the six-month-layoff clause and looked to the movies for employment. I had signed an agency contract for motion pictures with a Mr. Mayers, who assured me that his clients, although he personally didn't have an office in Hollywood, were being represented by the powerful and world-famous organization of Edington & Vincent. He told me of the existence of a lively correspondence between him and that worthy outfit that was going on in my behalf and how the "boys in Hollywood" were hopefully panting that my show would close so they could begin molding me into a movie star.

I bought a small roadster and drove West. The day after my arrival I presented myself at the impressive offices of Edington & Vincent. The building looked like the White House and the reception room like Grauman's Chinese. "What can I do for you?" asked a beautifully groomed secretary, who was protected by a glass partition from contact with visitors.

"I would like to see Mr. Edington."

"Do you have an appointment?"

"No."

"What's your name?" I told her.

"How do you spell that?"

"*S-L-E-Z-A-K.*"

"Sounds like a sneeze, doesn't it?"

"Yes, it does."

"What kind of name is that? Polish?"

"No, it's Czechoslovakian."

"Well, what do you know"—she showed her teeth—"live and learn!"

"Yes"—pause.

"Well, I don't know . . . You see, Mr. Edington is rather busy—what did you want to see him about?"

I began to lose my Continental charm. "Look here, dear lady," I said, still pleasant, "I will ask Mr. Edington if he wants you to know; and if he *does,* I'll tell you on my way out!" Then I added: "I am a client of the organization."

"Oh, but you couldn't be," she said, smiling. "Your photo isn't on the wall!"

Mr. Edington was polite. He asked me to sit down.

"So you're under contract to us, you say. Isn't that wonderful? Tell me, Mr. Slellsadge, what kind of stuff do you write?"

"I don't write," I answered, full of self-control. "I am an actor and singer. I just finished a long run on Broadway as one of the stars in Jerome Kern's *Music in the Air*. Mr. Mayers, my New York agent, told me that your firm represented his clients from New York here in Hollywood—"

"Wait a minute!" He looked disgusted. "You are with us on a *split-percentage deal?*"

I blushed. "I am afraid I am."

I was swiftly passed on to a Mr. Wolfenden, apparently a specialist in split-percentage deals. With great eloquence I told him who I was, all I had done professionally, and why I had come to Hollywood.

"You have an accent," he said reproachfully, and looked at me as the judge of the Westminster Kennel Show would look at a mongrel who was trying to compete with the pedigreed champions. Then he brushed away his concern. "Ah, what the hell," he said. "Tomorrow I have to go to Metro anway. Meet me at ten o'clock at the extras' entrance."

I didn't like the idea of entering Metro for the first time through the extras' entrance, but made up my mind I would be humble, do it their way, and see what would happen. So the next morning, I was there, conservatively dressed, and on time. Mr. Wolfenden and I walked through the gate; he waved to a uniformed policeman, and with a slight backward glance toward me and with his thumb thrown over his shoulder, he said, "He's with me."

Our first stop was at the office of a gentleman called Benny Thau. Mr. Wolfenden walked in, and I stood in the doorway fingering my spotless Panama hat and listened to their long, pointless conversation about the weather, parties, and poker games. When Mr. Wolfenden (Bill was his first name—and he insisted I call him that) was ready to leave, he spotted me still guarding the threshold. "Oh yeah, Benny, before I forget, this is Walter Sl—Sle—Slaa— What the hell is your name *anyway?*" I told him, making both syllables count.

"Well, anyhow, he's supposed to be hot stuff on Broadway. What do you think of him?"

Mr. Thau lifted his derrière about one inch off the chair with a slight forward movement, which I took as an invitation to shake hands. He asked me how long I had been in Hollywood. I told him: "Two days." He said, "Isn't that nice?" I said: "Yes." He asked me how I enjoyed the sunshine; I said: "Fine." He wanted to know if I played golf. I said that I did. He wanted to know what my handicap was. I said: "Forty-four." He said: "Ha, ha, that's very funny, but the main idea is to enjoy the game; the professionals really don't have any fun on the golf course, only the duffers." I said that I wouldn't know, as I had never been a professional. He chuckled. There was a pause. I then told him that I realized that he was a busy man, said good-by, and wished him good luck. He gratefully returned my sentiments, and Bill and I left.

The same pointless scene, with small variations in dialogue, happened in a few other offices—with the exception of the music department, where they knew my name because it was on the sheet music of *Music in the Air*. That cheered Bill considerably. He got quite expansive; explained Metro to me as if he owned it, showed me Marion Davies' bungalow (needless to say, from the outside), and pointed out the Irving Thalberg office.

"Thalberg," I said. "I'd like to meet *him*."

"Boy, now you're asking," was his guarded reply. With the same "Oh, what the hell, what can happen?" attitude we walked into that bungalow. The moment Mr. Wolfenden's frame appeared in the doorway, a secretary sprang to her feet and said with shrill authority: "Mr. Wolfenden, will you PLEASE—*CALL* for an appointment. Mr. Thalberg is *NOT IN*." While she was talking, a door on the left opened and the small, frail figure of Mr. Thalberg emerged. Bill plunged forward and said hurriedly: "Oh, Mr. Thalberg, I would like you to meet Mr. Slezak." (This time he got my name right.) Mr. Thalberg, without stopping, called out a pleasant how-do-you-do and disappeared through another door. Bill beamed with pride, slapped me on the back, and explained: "Boy, are you lucky! You met Thalberg!"

The next time I saw Mr. Thalberg was a few months later. I had more or less given up on my efforts to break into the movies, and resigned myself to sitting out my enforced idleness.

One day while I was playing golf, putting on the eleventh green, a car with a loud-speaker drove up, paging me. "Important message at the clubhouse—call Ben Piazza, casting director at Metro." I outran the caddy to the clubhouse and got on the phone. Ben was quivering with excitement. "Walter, we have THE part for you. Mr. Thalberg wants to see you right away."

I broke every speed law in getting there; Mr. Piazza was glowing with the joy of a happy giver of presents. He got Mr. Thalberg on the phone, and with the reverent attitude of the Moslem bowing toward Mecca said: "Mr. Slezak is in my office." Then he sprang to his feet. "Let's go." And we raced across the lot.

"What's it all about?" I asked, unable to bear the suspense any longer.

"HE will tell you," was all I could get from him.

We were ushered right into Mr. Thalberg's high-domed inner sanctum, a tremendous desk at the end of the room, reminiscent of Mussolini's office. Mr. Thalberg sat at the desk holding a telephone to his ear and making notes. He motioned for us to come forward—all the while talking into the phone—until we were standing about five feet away from his desk. He then looked up and abruptly waved us away, and pantomimed for us to leave his office. We backed out, rather bewildered. Mr. Piazza, a very nice man whom I had known when he was an agent in New York, tried in every way to relieve his and my embarrassment. He explained how busy Mr. Thalberg was, what tremendous responsibility he carried on his frail shoulders, that he was probably talking long distance, etc.

We waited and waited. I noticed that other people went into the holy shrine and came out again and I began to grow indignant. I walked over to the secretary and told her that I insisted upon seeing Mr. Thalberg right away; that I was called away from a golf course and on that particular day I had been playing rather well; that I refused to be treated in such a manner; that I had missed lunch and that unless she announced me instantly I would walk in unannounced. She gave me the cold fish-eye, picked up the phone, and said: "Mr. Piazza and a man are still waiting."

A minute later Mr. Thalberg came out of the room. He was very nice and polite to me. "I am so sorry we bothered you. You see, we are casting the part of a Viennese composer: I was told that you have an accent and that you are a good pianist, but I was *not* told that you are a young man: the part calls for an actor of at least seventy."

One day I called my agents' office to find out if anything was doing, if they knew of a job for me. The girl on the switchboard said:

"Oh, but you are no longer with us, Mr. Slezak! Mr. Edington sold your contract to the Swinburn Agency. *Do* get in touch with them. Good luck!"

Now I really was baffled. Why would anybody buy my contract? I was certainly not a hot property. But Mr. Swinburn was honest and told me. It seemed that he and Mr. Edington were indulging in the great California pastime of golf and got bored playing for money. So they began betting their unimportant clients on each hole. I was lost on a putt on the seventh green.

Ernst Lubitsch, whom I had known from my early days in Berlin, gave a big party to celebrate Max Reinhardt's spectacular production of *Midsummer Night's Dream* at the Hollywood Bowl. (In 1935 it was made into a movie, and I well remember the elegant souvenir programs that had William

Shakespeare's head, gold-embossed in raised profile on one side, and Jack Warner's head on the other.)

Supper was in the playroom. I was seated at a table with Myron Selznick, the agent, Herbert Marshall, the great English actor, Gloria S. (who was then engaged to Marshall) and a writer, M.L., who was quite drunk. Gloria S. wore a lovely low-cut dress with little flowers on the rim of her décolletage. M.L. tried to pick these flowers. Miss S. made a brave effort to be a good sport about it, and Herbert Marshall was also very valiant, whispering: "Come on, old chap, cut it out!" Well, a flower must have fallen into the décolletage, and M.L. tried to retrieve it. That was too much for good Herbert, who hissed: "You dirty dog!" M.L. quietly got up, lifted one side of the table and turned it over, spilling everything from fruit salad to champagne on the innocent bysitter, Mr. Selznick. And before anyone could stop him, he stepped over to Mr. Marshall, who was still seated, and knocked him out of his chair.

Herbert Marshall had lost a leg during the First World War, and though he gets around very well and manages admirably, it is not easy for him to defend himself in a fight. I became enraged, lifted M.L. with my strong arms, and carried him, kicking and struggling, into the garden. The wife of M.L. materialized, understandably dismayed, and cried: "Please put him down. After all, he is a gentleman!"

"He didn't behave like one," was my grandiose retort. And I threw him in the pool.

When I returned to the playroom, I found bedlam. Lubitsch, the unfortunate host, was wrestling with Ali Hubert, trying to prevent him from going into the garden. Hubert was afflicted with a clubfoot and knew what it meant to be physically handicapped. He was swinging a full bottle of beer and announced that he would kill that son of a bitch M.L. Lubitsch begged him not to. Back at our table an eager group of people were cleaning up Mr. Selznick, removing assorted viands and goodies from his person. Still on the floor and unable to get up was Mr. Marshall, unable to get up because Marlene Dietrich was draped over him, comforting him with a tiny lace handkerchief and imploring him over and over: "Speak to me, Bart, speak to me!"

"Please let me get up! I am perfectly all right, if you just let me get up!" was all poor embarrassed Bart could say.

Mady Christians, the tall, blond statuesque actress, was restraining petite Gloria, who announced at the top of her voice *what* she would do to M.L. (painful and most degrading). And in the corner of the room stood Max Reinhardt, observing the scene with quiet detachment and said: "*Indianer!*"

After all the tempers had cooled, great efforts were made to affect reconciliations, and everybody gave his most solemn word of honor that nothing of the deplorable incident would be leaked to the press.

As was to be expected, the next morning, there were blazing headlines, including a very aloof statement of M.L. "that Mr. Marshall had made a remark to him, but had failed to smile."

Around noon the following day, I received a call from Paramount to come right over and talk to a Mr. Antonescu. I was all packed and ready to leave for New York, having been signed by Gilbert Miller for a show with Ina Claire. Nevertheless, I rushed over to Paramount, where I was royally received. As an opener I mentioned that I was about to go back East for a new play. Mr. Antonescu said: "Then let's make a sound tract of your voice right away. We won't need a photographic test—we see what you look like. (The last was said as a joke.) But if you wait until four-thirty, you can sing with an orchestra."

I was puzzled. "What do you want me to sing?"

"Oh, anything you like—*Bohème, Tosca, Lohengrin* . . ."

"But that's grand opera," I laughed. "I haven't got that kind of voice."

"Oh, come now, Mr. Slezak"—he poked me in the ribs—"if you can sing it for the Metropolitan, you can sing it for Paramount."

Then it dawned on me, slowly and beautifully. They were mistaking me for my father. I started probing around and finally got the whole story: Grace Moore had just made a tremendous success in *One Night of Love,* and all studios were looking for opera stories and opera singers who looked human. During a story conference a very elderly gentleman sighed: "What we need is a voice like Slezak's. I heard that man at the Metropolitan—oh, how he brought down the house." Then he got up and went to the men's room. While he was gone, somebody said: "Slezak is in Hollywood. He was involved in that big melee at Lubitsch's house last night. Let Casting get in touch with him."

After just having spent five months knocking on closed doors, I truly enjoyed how Mr. Antonescu tried to sell me on the idea of working for Paramount. "If we want you," he assured me, "we will buy up your stage contract. You can forget about your commitment."

When at last I disclosed my poor, miserable identity—that I was NOT the opera singer Slezak, but his son, and had sung only in musical comedies, he at first refused to believe it. Then he checked with the very elderly gentleman, who had long since emerged from the men's room, and learned that the year he had heard Slezak sing at the Met was 1910.

Ode to Liberty was the name of the play Sidney Howard had adapted from the French hit *Liberté Provisoire.* Ina Claire, a beautiful, enchanting woman, a brilliant actress, and one of the great and true stars of the American theater, didn't like the third act of our play and wanted it rewritten. She kept saying to me: "Don't learn the third act—it will all be changed." But Sidney Howard had a mind of his own and didn't agree and repeatedly said so. I believed him and learned my lines, but Ina didn't. Our first performance was in Princeton, where Sidney Howard was a professor. Ina got frantic with opening-night jitters and refused to go on. After lengthy negotiations held through the door of her bathroom, where she had locked herself in, a compromise was affected. Sidney Howard stepped before the curtain and told the audience that Miss Claire didn't feel that she was ready to give the kind of performance that was expected of her, but he invited the audience to stay and regard the show like a dress rehearsal. He also promised them that their money would be refunded. Later on, he told me that, as he was talking, he had a vision of college boys crawling around the floor, picking up discarded stubs, and later redeeming them.

The show went reasonably well, except for the last act, where our lovely Ina was very shaky with her lines. So we resorted to prompters—one sitting in the fireplace, one with a flashlight under the table covered by a long tablecloth, one in each of the wings, and pinned to my vest was the text of a love scene. When the scene came up, I turned my back to the audience, threw back my lapels, and Ina read the whole scene off my manly chest.

After the show, we all went to Sidney Howard's house and there, sitting quietly in a corner, was Albert Einstein. I've a highly developed sense for the historic and was conscious of WHAT he represented in the world of science. I was overawed to be sitting on the same sofa with the greatest man since Isaac Newton. We spoke German, and he was grateful that I didn't ask him to explain the theory of relativity. Because nearly everybody else at the party did just that; and his feeble answer was:

"Vell, you see, it's rahder difficult . . ."

We talked about Berlin, the wonderful city it was before Hitler took over; we talked a great deal about music, and he mentioned that he was basically a very lazy man; that when he had to tackle some particularly difficult problems he always found dozens of excuses to postpone the work: clearing out his desk, looking through his clothes for small change, and convincing himself that he had to practice the violin. But when he reached that stage, his wife gently took the violin away from him, and then he knew that he'd have to settle down to serious work.

Being basically a very lazy man myself, I knew what he meant and was proud and gratified to have something in common with Albert Einstein. After about half an hour, the conversation lagged. He had nothing more to say to me, and I couldn't think of anything bright, except to stare at him in admiration. But I felt the need to keep the conversation going, no matter how, because this was a historic moment in my life. So I told him a joke:

A few orthodox Jews, all from different villages in Poland, were arguing which one boasted the greatest *Wunder Rabbi*. Many examples were cited, until Moishe spoke up:

"OUR *Wunder Rabbi* is the greatest! The *miracles* this man performed! He saw a man, completely lame, leaning on his crutches: 'Lift your left arm,' he commanded, 'and throw the crutch away.'

The man obeyed and fell on the ground on his left side. They propped him up and the rabbi said: "Now throw your right crutch from you." And the man fell on the ground on his right side. Again they propped him up, and the rabbi said, with thunder in his voice: "Now take *both* your crutches and throw them from you." And the man slowly raised both his arms, threw away both crutches, and fell flat on his face!

"*Nu?*" asked one of the Jews.

"*I saw it!*" screamed Moishe. "*I saw it with my own eyes!*"

Professor Einstein thought for a long time, then looked at me, with great innocent blue eyes, and said, "But that isn't a miracle!"

A few years later, I wrote to him about my collection of original manuscripts and hinted that he was not represented in my gallery of immortals. By return mail he sent me a handwritten page of the original theory of relativity, which is now one of the prides of my collection.

Of all the different media of show business, I found radio the hardest to crack. Radio in the thirties was a holy conspiracy, controlled by a small group of people whose main purpose, so it seemed to me, was to exclude outsiders in general, and me in particular. Forty or fifty actors did 95 per cent of all the work.

The fact that I had by then successfully starred in several Broadway shows meant nothing. I had to audition like anyone else, most of the time for assistant secretaries, who sat in their soundproof control room, like mermaids in an aquarium, carrying on animated conversations among themselves and paying no attention whatsoever to the poor slobs who stood in the studio and acted into the microphone. There is a joke about an eager young psychoanalyst who asks his professor: "Isn't it terribly tiring and strenuous to listen all day long to the patients' stories?" The professor shrugs his shoulders. "Who listens!" In the thirties, we told that joke about the casting directors.

But at a party, I met a radio director and he gave me my first radio job. It was a Christmas show, and I portrayed Herr Gruber, the man who wrote, "Silent Night, Holy Night." I plucked around on the zither, desperately groping for the tune, and had to say to my wife (in heavy German accent):

"*Liebling*, I hav a bootiful melody inside me—but I can't get it out!"

"Trrry Karl, trrry . . ." she answered. "You *must* get it out."

"I *am* trying, *Mein Liebling*, but I can't get it out." After a few more attempts on the zither to get it out, I finally did, and the tune emerged. After having played the first six bars, my wife began to sing it—never explaining how she knew the melody AND the lyrics.

Then the announcer stepped to the mike. "And that's how one of the great songs of the world was born!"

"And remember, folks," he continued, "that guy never got a penny of royalties."

My next job was for "RINSO WHITE" and in my chest of memories I treasure the wonderful commercial.

The announcer opened the show and said:

"Today, folks, let's go and talk to a famous lady!" (Footsteps, produced by the sound man.) "Well, Mona, what are you smiling about?"

A woman's voice with an Italian accent answered: "I got a lot to smile about; I know about Rinso!"

"Now, isn't that amazing; Mona Lisa, who hangs in the Louvre, in Paris, France, knows about Rinso."

"Tell us, Mona, how come?"

The Italian voice answered: "The other day, two American women were admiring me, and one said: (Now we got two Middle Western voices.) "Why, Gladys, where did you get your snow-white hands?" "But Mabel, haven't you heard about Rinso . . . ?" and they delivered the whole dreary commercial.

Triumphantly the announcer concluded: "And that's how popular Mona Lisa, who hangs in the Louvre in Paris, France, knows about Rinso."

I was flat on my face with laughter, but got disapproving looks from everybody else. They were all congratulating each other on that wonderful new angle of doing a commercial.

I finally managed to get on a serial. It was *So Big,* by Edna Ferber. The producer called me to audition, together with eight other actors, all for the same part. We had to talk in a Pennsylvania Dutch accent. I listened around and found out the other contestants weren't any more familiar with Pennsylvania Dutch than I was. So when my turn came, I made up an accent of my own, using several German dialects, as I imagined they would sound in English.

"What kind of an accent is that?" a guy in the control room called out. He sounded surprised.

"Amish!" I answered with a straight face. "I used to *live* there!"

I got the job.

Every big Hollywood studio, so I was then informed, had its favorite actors' agent, a fellow with whom the big bosses especially enjoyed doing business. I never found out what qualifications a man has to have to become a favorite agent. Some say he has to be able to lose in gin rummy and poker—to the right people. Others claim that he has to give kickbacks on his commissions, and there are still others who will tell you that he must—at all times—have on hand a ready supply of attractive starlets, endowed with high ambitions and low morals. I am sure that all this is a calumny, and I personally don't believe a word of it.

But when Fox announced that they were going to film *Music in the Air,* I asked questions and learned that the favorite agent for that studio was a man who called himself Colonel Sharp and that he lived at the Beverly Wilshire Hotel.

I called on him at noon, and he received me, lying in bed,

wearing a hat and smoking a cigar. I explained that I was anxious for him to get me the same part I had played on Broadway in the movie version.

"Whatta you talking about?" He glared at me. "You didn't play that part on Broadway?"

"Of course I did."

"Like *hell* you did!" He shifted his cigar to another part of his face. "Look here, kid, don't hand me any bull! Hollywood may be three thousand miles away from New York but we know what's going on. Now I happened to be at the opening of that show, and I certainly didn't see you in it."

At first I was speechless, then I grew eloquent with fury. I reached for the phone and asked for Jerome Kern's apartment. He was staying at the same hotel, and he answered right away. I shoved the phone into the colonel's hand and said: "Ask him!"

"Do you know a guy called Slezak?"

"Never heard of him!" said Kern, thinking it was a gag, and hung up.

"Beat it!" said the colonel, and I left.

On September 26, 1933, Papa sang *I Pagliacci* at the Vienna Opera House. He was then sixty years old.

"I felt like a twenty-five-year-old," he wrote me. "My voice sounded as young as ever, without any strain or effort. It was one of those rare evenings and the spark of my happiness must have jumped across the footlights and the orchestra pit into the audience. Rarely have I had such an ovation after the aria 'Ridi Pagliacci.' They applauded right through the intermission. As I was waiting for my second-act entrance, I thought: Wouldn't that be a wonderful way to leave, to end my career in opera on such a high note; maybe I will never be able to sing so well! By the time the final curtain had rung down, my mind was made up. I had sung my last opera! When Mama came to the dressing room, glowing with happiness and pride at her 'Old Man,' I took her face in my hands and said, 'Lieserl, tonight I have sung for the last time—that was my good-by!' We both had a good cry, and the next morning, I called on Clemens Krauss, the general manager, and informed him that I had retired. 'But that's impossible, that's unheard of,' he protested. 'You cannot simply walk away from a career such as yours without giving at least a farewell performance.' 'My dear Herr Director,' I laughed, 'I don't go to other people's funerals; I am certainly not going to my own.'"

A few weeks later Papa got an official document from Chancellor Dollfuss, informing him that he would receive the highest decoration the state of Austria can bestow on a civilian, and that the ceremony of presentation would be held on the stage of the Opera House, the place of his great triumphs, surrounded by all his colleagues, the orchestra, and assorted functionaries.

So Papa wrote him a very nice letter, thanking him for the great honor: ". . . but, Your Excellency, I know how these official interments are handled: I have attended a few of them myself!

"It's eleven in the morning, everybody has to appear, dressed in cutaway or something equally uncomfortable. The 'dear departing one' is led up an elevated platform and seated on a 'throne' that had been brought up from the property room, dusted and decorated with laurel leaves. Then begin the speeches: I will be informed that my name will be entered into the illustrious annals of the Vienna Opera House as one of their immortals, that my contribution will never be forgotten and that the memory of my performances will live on as an inspiration to coming generations of singers! Believe me, Your Excellency, it's the bunk! The other tenors are already waiting in the wings and the annals are read by nobody. The singer is a torchbearer: as long as the torch burns brightly, the crowd will follow him. Once it's extinguished, he is alone. But I am just sentimental enough to get very emotional and possibly burst out in tears, and I would like to spare you and me that spectacle. Permit me to come to your office, where you will hand me the greatly appreciated medal; I will tell you a few good stories and that will be it!"

Dollfuss wrote back: "All right, if that's the way you want it!" Clemens Krauss and Papa rode to the chancellery. At the presentation, the chancellor, who was a tiny man and reached just up to Papa's navel, said: "Herr Kammersaenger, I hope you will forgive me, but I cannot just hand you that medal; I will have to say a few words." He then began a speech and inadvertently slid into the phrase about the annals, then the never-to-be-forgotten contributions and the inspiration to coming generations. Suddenly, all burst out laughing. Dollfuss gave Papa the box with the medal. "Go home," he said, "you are incorrigible." Then Papa asked that the newspapers should not be informed of his retirement because "when they write the obituary, one usually learns all the things one didn't do well, and I am not curious."

Somehow I sensed what later was to become firm knowledge—that an actor in America never has a position. At best, he has a job. And I never felt secure enough to get my own apartment. Even after *Music in the Air* was firmly entrenched as a solid hit, I only sublet a suite at the Hotel St. Moritz. Friends of mine had left for Europe and elected me as foster parent for their fox terrier and parrot. The parrot loved me; he sat on my shoulder and nibbled on my ear. All he could say when he began life with me was: *"Oi, is duz a leben,"* and when there was a knock at the door, he said: "So, come in already." Where he had learned his Yiddish I was never able to discover, as my friends who left him with me were Mormons. The fox terrier hated me and nipped at my feet whenever he could. And when he had really hurt me, he pretended he was only playing. I bought a canary bird, who didn't even say peep, much less sing. A complaint to the pet shop disclosed that I had failed to ask what sex my bird was and thus had been sold a female. But the man was very helpful; he sold me a male and one more female. And a breeding cage with three partitions, the center to be occupied by the male and the sides by the ladies. After about a week, I was to assume that their acquaintance had graduated into friendship and the partition was to be removed. Then I was to place two wire baskets into each corner and a box with nesting wool in the center. It turned out to be a most happy menage: their polygamy flourished and soon they began building nests, and the day the first egg was laid I passed out cigars.

With a small silver spoon so as not to touch it with human scent, I carefully removed each egg and replaced it with an artificial one, hoping the lady birds wouldn't notice the deception. The real eggs I kept in a small box on a bed of cotton, and after they had stopped laying for two days, I returned the originals, and such hatching you have never seen, the father feeding the ladies and personally sitting whenever the girls felt like knocking off for a while. Eleven eggs were hatched, and I took turns feeding the little ones. Out of the yellow of a hard-boiled egg and some corn meal I made a paste and with a toothpick I smeared that into their gaping beaks. When the birds grew bigger, I bought another, very large cage, but the birds were tame and preferred to fly around. They retained their perch only at night, but not one of them sang. So the man in the pet shop, who took great interest in my project and sold me several books on the raising of canaries, was able to purchase for me a mechanical singing teacher. A larger metal cylinder filled with water was covered by another, tightly fitting cylinder whose weight pressed out the air and into a tiny whistle that produced the trills and rolls of accepted canary songs. I had the damned thing on for eight hours a day but I must have raised a family of deaf mutes. The only one who learned to sing was the parrot.

Then some demented girl friend gave me a little Easter bunny. I lived in constant fear that the unpleasant fox terrier might be a rabbit fancier, and the rabbit shared that fear, so I made him live in the bathtub. He couldn't get out, but one evening while I was in the theater, a new hotel maid came into the apartment, was confronted with fourteen canaries flying around, a screeching parrot, a growling terrier, and she fled, leaving the door to the bathroom open.

When I returned that evening, the room clerk at the desk handed me a letter from the management. It began: "After all, Mr. Slezak . . ." I didn't bother to read on. Next day I borrowed a small shovel and buried the rabbit in Central Park. The fox terrier I placed in a kennel, bought fourteen small bird cages, and so was able to give the birds away. I kept the parrot and moved to the Warwick Hotel, hoping they wouldn't learn about my past as a zoologist.

By 1936 I became landed gentry. Lured by a real estate ad promising that on a small, rarely traveled country road I would come upon a woodsy place of great beauty, nestling against a hill in the midst of a casually landscaped acre of trees and evergreens, I set out to find my *buen retiro*.

The small country road was so rarely traveled that I spent two hours finding it. After I did, I came upon a beguiling wooden structure that had no cellar, no basement, and had most certainly not been planned: like a game of Scrabble, it must have happened!

On top of several large rocks perched a cubelike form, nine feet long, eight feet wide, and seven feet high. It had two small windows, one door that opened up to a five-foot drop to the ground, and another door with two steps rising to a coal stove that all but blocked the entrance to the "living room" (nine by thirteen). Three more steps led down to what I recognized to be the kitchen. Long and narrow, six by fourteen, to be precise, it featured an enormous sink out of which proudly rose a water pump. Next to it a huge wood stove; facing it, and making passage between them difficult, was an ancient icebox. The floor of the kitchen slanted to conform to the contour of the ground below. Leaning against one wall, but not connected to the inside of the house by a door, was a large porch with lattice on three sides and bird's-nests under the roof.

Thirty yards away, set on a knoll, with a breath-taking view of the majestic Westchester hills and the Croton Reservoir —clear to the spire of the Empire State Building—stood a twin-seater outhouse.

I was enchanted and rented it on a long lease for three hundred dollars a year.

Opening a door in the house sounded like stepping into *Inner Sanctum.* But it was a haven of privacy: no one could phone me, no one could find me, unless I passed out elaborate directions. I soon became a wizard with the stoves. I learned to look a kerosene lamp in the eye without flinching, and I rigged up an elaborate flashlight attachment along the path to the outhouse.

As the "mansion" had stood vacant for about a year, my first chore was to evict various animals of the forest who claimed squatter's rights. Squirrels under the roof, rats under the house, and mice in the drawers. A friend who had connections with the Bronx Zoo presented me with a garter snake. I named her Bella, and she took care of the mice in no time. In fact, she became quite tame and stayed around the house. Every fall, when the weather got too cold, I caught her, and she spent the winter at the reptile house in the zoo. I became dearest friend to the hardware people of Mount Kisco; they sold me their entire stock of rattraps and poisons.

Outside the house there was another pump, so I rigged up a barrel into one of the trees, pumped it full of water, and thus had my shower bath. I also owned a collapsible rubber bathtub, built a shelter for my car, and soon had the nicest weekend shack a bachelor who loved to rough it could have.

One night, during the Broadway run of *Music in the Air,* a very nice man had come backstage. He was very complimentary about my performance, said he was a motion-picture director, and promised that someday he would have a great part for me. The nice gentleman was the famous Leo McCarey. A few years later, when I played in *Ode to Liberty* with Ina Claire, and again when I was in Sigmund Romberg's *May Wine,* he came backstage. Every time, he assured me: "I'll have a great part for you someday." It became a running gag.

In December 1941 I experienced the lowest low in my checkered career. After a three weeks' run on Broadway my show, *The Little Dark Horse,* closed. It was a comedy about miscegenation that had gone over very big in Westport and very small in New York. It was my first Broadway flop. I was blue and way down in the dumps. Pearl Harbor had just happened, and I began to feel a certain antagonism and resentment of my Austrian background among many of my acquaintances. All means of communication with my parents, who were then in Bavaria, had been severed, and the only way to let each other know that we were alive and well was Red Cross messages of fifteen words—every six months.

Then a producer sent me a play. I read it, but the lead was a dashing Barrymore type, for which I would have been dead wrong. I called back and learned that the producer didn't want me for the lead, but thought that I might consider the role of the gardener, an insignificant supporting part.

"Walter," he said, "I know you haven't worked much this year. Your last play was a flop. I thought of doing you a favor."

I was rather rude and hung up in a huff. Then I sat down and took stock of my career and my future. Could it be possible that my reputation and position in the theater had deteriorated to such an extent in one short year that I was being considered for such a small part. Unfortunately, an actor never correctly knows his true standing at a given moment. Maybe I was all washed up, and he WAS trying to do me a favor. I made up my mind to call him back and apologize. And, just to stall an unpleasant call, I leafed through my little phone book. There I found the name and number of an Isidor Oblo. I dialed.

"Mr. Oblo," I began, "I find your name in my telephone book, but I have no idea who gave it to me or who you are. I am curious. What do you do?"

"I am an astrologer," was the reply.

My eyes lit up: I hadn't had a good astrologer since I left Europe. I quickly gave him date and place, hour and minute of my birth, and the following day I sat in his study.

This is what he said: "You have gone through a very bad period, but it's getting better. During the first week of January, you will be involved in a scandal with a woman but it will blow over and not harm you. Around the middle of February, you will be offered a job—it's kind of an odd job—it has *something* to do with your profession—it won't mean much in itself, but take that job. It will start you traveling and by May 15, you'll be rid of all your worries and an entirely new career will begin for you."

I went home and waited. The scandal came—and it was a dilly while it lasted—but it blew over and didn't harm me. On February 13 an agent, Jane Broder, called. "Walter, I don't know if you'd be interested," she said. "It's kind of an odd job!" (When she said ODD JOB, both my ears snapped up and stood at attention.) "The university in Austin, Texas, wants a professional Broadway actor to play the star part in Molière's

Bourgeois Gentilhomme, with the student body. He'll have to give a talk on Molière. The money isn't much–"

"Never mind," I yelled into the phone, "I'll do it!" Two weeks later I arrived in Austin with a strep throat, a temperature of 104, and eleven pages of notes on Jean Baptiste Poquelin, professionally known as Molière, 1622 to 1673.

A new translation of *Le Bourgeois Gentilhomme* had been made by a member of the faculty; she had updated the dialogue into colloquial English. Sentences like "You said it, kiddo!" and "It's O.K. by me" sounded strange at first, but how much stranger did they sound when they were delivered in a soft, lazy Southern drawl. Harmless, nice young people were dressed in the period of 1650, long curly wigs and all, and they were mincing about in what they had been led to believe was the grand manner. It was pretty horrible, and I began to doubt Mr. Oblo, because he had said very distinctly that the job had *something* to do with my profession. Being naturally tactful, I loudly voiced my opinions and was not elected Prince Charming of the campus. There also developed a smoldering feud between the music and the drama departments of the university, because the music department insisted on playing the entire Lully score –*uncut!* Lully is *not* a hilarious composer and can be taken only in small doses and even *then* only very good musicians are able to make it bearable. But a fifty-two-minute rendition, conscientiously plowed through by an earnest, well-meaning student orchestra, just managed to spread a numbing layer of boredom over the audience. We, the actors on the stage, were not very mirth-provoking either, and thus gave that layer of boredom a firm second coat. As I felt that we were dying on our feet, I tried to hoke it up a little, but was severely reprimanded by the faculty, who felt that levity and laughter were not compatible with the dignity of Molière.

My frustration and irritation were aggravated by a song that was so popular then that it was all but impossible to evade it. Morning, noon, and night wherever one went, at breakfast, on the campus, on the street, over the radio, out of every room—there it was—like the Chinese torture—blaring in one's ears: "Clap, clap clap clap—Deep in the Heaaaaart—of Texas!" Molière has since become to me synonymous with Austin, Texas.

One night I returned to my hotel and found a wire from Hollywood waiting for me: "Could place you in an excellent part with two outstanding stars and prominent director at top studio stop can we handle your business." It was signed by one of the big talent agencies.

I was then, as the saying goes "without picture representation" and rushed to the Western Union office to wire my enthusiastic YES. There I was handed three more wires that had just come in, all from actors' agents, wanting to handle me. I realized then that the call was out for me, but who would want me so badly? The mystery was cleared up by a fifth wire: "Leo McCarey wants you for Ginger Rogers-Cary Grant picture at RKO. Signed Gardner Agency." So Mr. McCarey remembered ten years later. Ben Piazza, who was by then casting director at RKO, called me about coming to the coast for a screen test. I knew enough about studio procedures to realize that they never invest even one dollar in train fare without an option agreement. So I magnanimously declined his offer to pay for my fare to Hollywood, mentioning that I was coming out there anyway. He was very pleased. He had saved the studio money.

And I was ecstatic with pleasure, especially because my engagement at the university was drawing to a close. I left there—unloved, unmourned, and, I hope, unremembered.

Three men have been placed by the good Lord in my path—to point the way and give direction: Mike Curtiz, who started me in pictures, J. J. Shubert, who brought me to America, and

Leo McCarey, who started me on the road to modest riches. I retain great affection and feelings of gratitude for all three of them. Especially to Leo McCarey, whom I have honored beyond his wildest dreams by partly naming my son, Leo, after him (95 per cent after my father, the great Leo, and 5 per cent after Leo, the great McCarey).

A few days before my scheduled screen test, Jack Gardner, who had become my agent, called with the news that RKO wanted me to sign an option contract, which they might pick up if they liked my test. I knew a little bit about salaries in Hollywood and considered the money they offered ridiculous. I went to Lubitsch for advice.

"If they *want* you—they'll pay you three thousand dollars a week without blinking an eye—and if they *don't* want you, you can offer to work for *thirty* dollars a week, and they won't *touch* you."

So I stood pat, but RKO issued an ultimatum: agree to our proposal or we will call off the screen test. Stubborn by nature and fortified by my belief in Mr. Oblo's predictions, I bought a return ticket to New York and called Leo McCarey to say good-by. He was also the producer of the film and had not been told that the front office had called off the test. "Let me talk to them," he said. "I'll call you back in ten minutes." Three minutes later the phone rang:

"Tomorrow, 9 A.M., Stage 7, ready to shoot," he said, and added: "Don't be nervous and good luck!"

The next day, I made my test, and the following day—rather than sit around and stare at the phone—I played thirty-six holes of golf. Back at the clubhouse there was a message for me that had been telephoned in by my old Viennese aunt, with whom I was staying: "Go to RKO and *sing!*" Oh, my God, not again, I thought. I was puzzled and worried. I had so expected a positive yes.

In the parking lot at RKO, I ran into Sheridan Gibney,

who was writing the scenario. "Just saw your test," he shouted. "Congratulations! So glad you'll be with us."

I ran through the gate and kissed the uniformed policeman. Then I walked into McCarey's office. "A double scotch, please," I begged, and my legs buckled with joy.

The message, I later learned, was to read: "Go to RKO—and sign!" Ah, these Viennese telephones. And by May 15 I had signed a contract for two pictures a year—with NO loan-outs, for five years.

I owe a debt of gratitude to many friends and colleagues who—before me—trekked the exhilarating road from the Broadway stage to the pearly gates of Hollywood. Proudly clutching a seven-year contract, starting at seven hundred fifty a week, they stepped off the train and happily started out by buying a new car. They rented an elegantly furnished house in a choice location, hired servants, a gardener, indulged in a little landscaping, and opened charge accounts at Magnin's and Saks. Then they went on exciting shopping sprees replenishing their wardrobes and acquiring the kind of clothes that are indigenous to Southern California and the movie colony.

There would always be clever old-timers who would explain that the best way to get ahead in Hollywood was by playing the social game. "Go out, be seen, be fun—mingle with the important wheels, make friends!"

Unfortunately, playing the social game inevitably leads to "entertaining." And "entertaining" is a bottomless pit. It will start out harmlessly enough with a home-cooked meal, then progress to a goulash party on the lawn with a keg of beer—and winds up with caterers, a horde of waiters and kitchen help, a tent, a dance band and a dance floor covering the swimming pool, and a staggering liquor bill.

Most actors have tremendous trust and faith in their professional ability and feel that all they really need is the "one lucky break." And that hopeful optimism often represses the cold brutal fact that nearly all seven-year contracts contain a six-month-option clause.

IF, during that first option period, the studio failed to find the right part for you;

IF whatever role you played has wound up on the cutting-room floor;

IF the cameraman did a heartless job of photographing you;

IF you had a bad director;

IF the fan magazines refused to show interest in you . . .

These and seven hundred fifty other IF's will, unexpectedly to you, bring about a telephone call from your agent: "Sweetheart, I got bad news for you! The studio didn't pick up your option!"

Very often a joke can ruin a career. A well-known European actress had signed a contract with MGM, who gave her a big build-up and made an extensive acting test of her. In it she played everything from stark tragedy to broad farce. The test was widely circulated in other studios. Sam Goldwyn saw it and exclaimed: "That woman is terrific—in a small way." Within twenty-four hours that remark was repeated all over Hollywood. The studio almost overnight lost all interest in her and she got the "Sweetheart, I got bad news" call.

The best thing in such a case is to count your losses quickly and get the hell back to New York, where it is not considered a disgrace to be unemployed and looking for a job.

I had learned from all this. So the day I signed with RKO, I returned to New York, sublet my apartment ONLY for the duration of the film, a ten-week guarantee. I put my harlequin great Dane in a boarding kennel. Then I got my old Buick out of the garage, changed the oil, checked the tires, and motored to the coast. There I rented a small studio apartment for eighty-five dollars a month. You see I remembered that after the First World War inflation was rampant in Europe and that only real estate had retained its value. I laid out my plans on the premise that this might be my first and last film, and I did not intend to let the money get away from me. I wanted to invest it in a farm that would provide an income and feed me if things got tough, so I wouldn't have to play "the role of the gardener." I had the farm all picked out. It was near New Hope, Pennsylvania, where, for many summers, I had graced the Bucks County Playhouse with my presence.

In our film, *Once upon a Honeymoon,* we had a Hungarian actress, Ferike Boros, who played Ginger Rogers' maid. She had a wonderfully warm and endearing personality—but she consistently blew her lines. Every time she got stuck, Leo McCarey made a big joke out of it, and we all laughed it up. He had worked with her before and knew that if she got tense and nervous her jolly, gay, and happy quality would not come through. And he was more interested in what showed on the film than in saving a few feet of negative.

To me Ferike was a windfall. I sat in a corner of the set and before every new take I prayed that she would blow. My mind worked like a computer: another scene blown, that's fifteen minutes, plus another fifteen minutes, and so on . . . add it up and translate it into shooting days. Add those to the ten-week guarantee. Prorate the days into salary, and the salary into money with which to buy additional acreage!

When Ferike's role was finished, my profit from her loss of memory was six and a half acres. They were fenced off and named "The Ferike Boros Pasture."

During the making of our film Cary Grant got married to Barbara Hutton. Leo admonished us all: "PLEASE, no jokes!" So I only gave him a bag with knickknacks from the five-and-ten and all was dignified. But when we left the studio, a fresh little newsboy stood at the gate, yelling at the top of his voice, "Cary Grant Hits Jackpot!"

I had known Cary many years ago in New York, when he was known as Archibald Leach and was straight man to a very funny burlesque comedian, Harry (Soup) Welch. To me, Cary is a marvel and my admiration for him is boundless. Not only has he been able to maintain the highest star status through twenty-seven years, but his performances grow and get better with every year. He can play anything from a sinister villain to the gayest charmer. May he wave for many, many more years.

It all happened at the Coronet Apartments on Sunset Boulevard. I was visiting Mme. Vera Schwarz, a dear friend of our family. She was a famous European soprano and had sung for many years with Papa at the Vienna Opera. She was now teaching.

Her phone rang. "All right, ask her to come up, please," she said, and bid me good-by, as she was expecting a new pupil—"a little Dutch girl"—who was coming for her first lesson. I took the elevator down, and when it had reached the lobby, I opened the door and stepped out. The date was August 8, the time 2:12 P.M., Pacific Standard Time.

Then God kissed me on both eyes! I blinked, opened them wide—and saw my wife.

36—25—34, 5 feet 3½ inches, 115 pounds, glove—6, shoes —5½, hair—light blond, eyes—blue. She was wearing a pink fuzzy Angora wool sweater. I held the door open for her. "Thank you," she said, and smiled with thirty-two faultless, beautifully matched teeth.

Her name was Johanna Van Rijn. She was born in Holland, and when she was two years old, her parents moved to the Dutch East Indies. She spoke English, German, French,

Italian, Dutch—and Malay. She had begun to take singing lessons, while still in the East, but when the war broke out, she came to the university at Baton Rouge to study with the famous Pasquale Amato, a colleague of my father's at the Met. Then Amato had died, and she came to Hollywood to study with Vera Schwarz. It was as simple as that.

A week later, I high-pressured Mme. Schwarz to give a party inviting me and the little Dutch girl together. Around ten o'clock I suggested that we leave and go to the Players Restaurant. We sat on the terrace. Never before was I so blissfully content and happy just to be with someone; she was so genuine, so completely natural—with not an ounce of pretense or phoniness; I felt like coming home to a place I had always known, where everything was familiar and good, solid and clean. I had worked all day and was tired and didn't feel like talking, so we asked for a deck of cards and sat there—playing gin rummy like an old married couple, until the candles on our table had burned out and the waiters stacked the chairs on the tables.

The following day, I sent the date of her birth to Isidor Oblo. One of the things he said was: "You won't know why, but you will be constantly elated in each other's company."

For twenty years now, we have been elated, and the miracle of my parents' happy marriage has repeated itself in our life.

The film was finished, and I returned East to buy my farm and pick up my great Dane. I had received several communications from the kennel, expressing a keen desire to be rid of him. It seems that on a moonlit night he had somehow managed to break down the gate of his cage and chew his evil way into a cloistered enclosure that housed a giant French poodle and an Afghan hound, both thoroughbred bitches and both in heat. I am sure that he had a whale of a time, and he fathered an entirely new breed of four-legged monstrosities.

All my dogs always had a strong procreative urge. I once owned an English bulldog—seventy-six pounds of solid ugliness, slobbering, sniffling, and affectionate. One night, in Central Park, I let him run without a leash; he romped away and when I found him again, he was in the process of making violent love to a fox terrier bitch, a beautiful white clipped and groomed animal. While I was pondering whether or not to interrupt proceedings, a man came running along a path, whistling frantically and calling out: "Daisy, Daisy—where are you?"

"I am afraid Daisy is right here," I told him with a heavy heart. When the full impact of what was by now a *fait accompli* had hit him, he slowly turned to me—pale as a ghost—trembling. He said accusingly: "WHY ISN'T YOUR DOG MUZZLED?"

There was no point arguing with him!

I drove to Pennsylvania and bought "The Farm," a hundred eighty-six acres in rolling hills, picturesque as hell, and all buildings in good condition. I called it the Redhill Farm, after an ancient township. Then I drove back to New York to give up my apartment. I called several moving companies, but it was around October 1, and they were all busy; so I hired a couple of guys with a large truck, and together with the farm manager I had hired, we drove the eighty-four miles to the Redhill Farm. The truck was an old one and broke down several times. It was dark when we arrived; the "guys" wanted to get back to New York to their loved ones, so they simply dumped the whole stuff on the large porch, asked for overtime, and departed.

As the house had stood vacant for some time, electricity and gas were still disconnected. But I found a kerosene lamp from my old country estate in Kitchawan that still had some fuel left, pulled a mattress out from under the grand piano, got a few pillows from an old couch, and made my bed on the kitchen floor. Around two in the morning, I woke up—I wasn't used to such absolute silence—and stepped outside. It was a misty night, a half-moon shone through the haze. It reminded me of a Corot painting. I stood there and gazed at the two-hundred-fifty-year-old house, the large barn, the stables, corn-crib, sheds, the old smokehouse, and the fields and wooded hills. It was the first time in my life that I had owned land and suddenly a bond with Europe was severed. Whenever I had thought of "home," it had always been our house in Vienna or the estate in Tegernsee, but now THIS would be my anchor, to dig in and to grow roots. That night I grew up. I returned to my mattress with a serene feeling of security and accomplishment.

But when the morning sun crept through the unwashed, uncurtained windows and hit my eyes, things didn't look quite so serene any more. No hobgoblins had moved the furniture into the place while I was asleep. No imps had cleaned the house and the only "little people" that were around were a horde of stray cats who were scaring the living bejesus out of my great Dane. As I and the farm manager couldn't do it alone, I drove to "our town" for help. Our town was Ottsville, an unattractive little place, bisected by Route 611 and boasting a hardware store, general store, post office, and a Ford dealer. It also had a gas station that was out of gas most of the time. "Oh, you're the new city fella who bought one of our farms!" Hostility greeted me everywhere! It was impossible to find anybody locally, so I imported hired help from Trenton, thirty-four miles away.

Having gas and electricity connected took only six days. But getting a telephone was another thing. The only phone company that connected Ottsville and surrounding areas was a private one, owned by an old man and his wife. He serviced the poles, cables, and phones, and she was "the switchboard."

I had been tipped off that she was the real boss of the outfit and warned of her autocratic evil-tempered behavior. But never in my life have I been so rudely abused when I begged to have a phone installed. I got so furious that I threatened to complain to the American Telephone Company, foolishly assuming that they might have some sort of jurisdiction. I was given the horselaugh and the bum's rush.

Trembling with rage, I made up my mind to sell the farm again—even at a loss—and I canceled the rather large order for farm machinery that I had placed with the International Harvester dealer. So *he* descended on that nasty little monopoly and within two days they hung a wall phone in the kitchen and connected me to a party line of ten. One of the other nine was always talking. It was a joyous occasion when I picked up the phone and heard silence. But then the switchboard got on. "Oh, it's you," she said with vengeance in her voice, and my line went dead or I got six wrong numbers in a row, for which I was charged; or if I was being connected at all, I was cut off in the middle of my talk and was unable to crank the switchboard back into the sound of my outraged voice.

It took me years to learn that one has to own and live on a place for at least three generations to be so much as tolerated by the natives of Ottsville. To be *accepted* takes much longer and requires inbreeding.

They will shamelessly take advantage of a newcomer, and if that newcomer happens to be a Hollywood actor—no holds are barred. In the long run, I found it more economical to have plumbers and electricians come forty-six miles from Philadelphia or eighty-four miles from New York than to hire local labor.

Luckily, RKO ordered me back to Hollywood to report for my next picture, *This Land Is Mine,* which starred the great Charles Laughton.

I had first seen Charles Laughton in *Payment Deferred* on Broadway. I saw the show seven times. I had known nearly all the great actors, Kainz, Bassermann, Werner Krauss, Raimu —to me, he topped them all. There is an expression in the German theater which indicates that an actor is especially talented and blessed: "He has God's telephone number in his pocket." Well, Laughton, I am sure, even has God's *unlisted* number. He can do just about anything—be hateful and lovable, frighten the hell out of you, break your heart or play comedy with an uncanny sense of timing. And all with the most wonderful diction and speech. I had then—and still have —a tremendous crush on him. I am his fan, in boundless admiration.

When I boarded the train in New York, I saw him standing on the platform, surrounded by friends, so I didn't introduce myself to him. But in Chicago, the following morning, where we had to change trains, I greeted him with a polite "Good morning." He swung around like a startled Baby Hippopotamus. "What do you want?" He sounded alarmed.

"Nothing, sir, nothing," I said. "Just wanted to wish you a good morning!" I was sorry that I had invaded his privacy. "I am an actor," I added, "and I will be in your next picture!"

His eyebrows shot up. "Are you a good actor?" He sounded apprehensive.

"BRILLIANT!" I replied, with mock grandeur.

His face widened into a wide grin: "Ah, a conceited son of a bitch!" And then very matter-of-factly: "Come on, let's have breakfast."

We had four or five hours to kill until the Chief left for California. "Do you know anything about paintings," he wanted to know. I admitted that I had studied for two years with Kuniyoshi at the Art Students League in New York. "Let's go to the Art Institute," was his decision.

Walking through a museum with Laughton is an unforgettable experience. On one hand, he has a profound knowledge and feeling for paintings and sculpture, and then again, he will employ the most obvious art dealer's phraseology. He rushed through a room filled with great masterpieces. "Don't look," he admonished me. "That's all bad." But at the end of the hall, he stopped before a small painting, and with his finger circled a spot of about three inches square. "THAT," he whispered reverently, "is REAL quality."

We stood before the large Seurat painting *A Sunday Afternoon on the Island of La Grande Jatte.* Laughton was dismayed. "It's badly hung," he moaned. "The light is all wrong." He made a guard roll down a corrugated door to shut out "that terrible glare." "The best point of view to see this work is from the floor," he said excitedly, and flopped down on the ground. "Come on, my boy, sit here," he commanded. I was a little embarrassed but obediently sat on the floor.

Meanwhile, lots of people who had recognized him stood around and watched us two lardy boys sitting there, and they pointed him out to newcomers who had drifted in from adjoining halls. "That's Charles Laughton—there on the floor—I don't know who the other one is!" The museum director rushed to greet his distinguished visitor. We got up with a little difficulty, I admit, and were shown some new acquisitions the museum had made. And again, I was amazed at the precise judgment and intelligent appreciation with which he discussed every detail.

We dined together on the train; and he became the great connoisseur of food and wine. He asked for *truite au bleu* and grouse with truffles, and perplexed the waiter no end. Then he began ordering wine: rare vintages which one *might* possibly find at Chambord, "21," or Voisin. The waiter, completely bewildered, just stared and kept on repeating: "We have Cresta Blanca, White, and we have Cresta Blanca, Red." Charles (I was by now permitted to call him that) bemoaned the lack of culinary culture and blamed it all on mass producing packaged food and on the uncivilized habit of drinking hard liquor before dinner, which immunizes the taste buds.

He told me that he had played Molière at the Comédie Française in Paris. So we talked French for a while. He speaks the most beautiful, perfect French, without a trace of an accent. He recited a scene from *Le Malade Imaginaire*. When he had finished, we both cried.

Then he became the great champion of the simple life in Southern California. He owned a house at Pacific Palisades, he told me, and upon awakening in the morning would often don an old pair of slacks, sandals, and an old straw hat and stroll down to the piers, where the fishing boats came in. There he would buy a few fish, walk back to his home, pick a few olives from his trees, press them for oil, and fry the fish. He was furious at the way many people spoil the wonderful avocado by filling it with crab meat, broiling it, or putting Thousand Island dressing on it—they should be eaten with just a little salt, or all their flavor and goodness disappear. (I agree with him.) He was full of praise for certain lesser-known California wines, displaying the full vintner's vocabulary.

I was entranced and fascinated because I began to realize that here was one of those rare people where truth and fiction, reality and imagination had completely fused, like water colors they had run together with the line of demarcation no longer visible. Here was a brilliant man and a glorious ham—and I use the word as the highest compliment: this man simply *had* to act, *had* to perform, *had* to be "on"—but not in the cheap and obvious way most comics are "on" all the time. Charles lived his fabulous life on a much more subtle and intelligent level. I know a lot of actors and they don't interest me very much; it never takes very long to find out what kind of mechanism is ticking inside. It's familiar to me. We will all act for the captain and the waiter in a restaurant, but Charles Laughton will give a full performance for the busboy who fills the glasses with water.

His knowledge of English, American, and French literature is baffling, and it takes only a minuscule amount of prodding to have him prove a point by a recitation. He is equally at home in the pages of the Bible, in the folios of Shakespeare, with Shaw, Brecht, and Racine.

Our conversation drifted to the film we were about to shoot. When I told him that I had the script with me on the train, he was very excited. "Please, oh please, let me read it," he begged. I was surprised that the star of the film had not been sent the screenplay and gave it to him before I retired.

Around one o'clock at night—I was already asleep—there was a knock at the door of my drawing room (paid for by RKO). Laughton stood outside, tears were streaming down his jowls. He held the manuscript in his hands: "Walter," he sobbed. "Oh, this is beautiful, so beautiful, the scope of it, the compassion, the understanding . . . listen," and he began to read. He acted all the roles (including mine, which at first didn't please me very much, but then he did it so well). A torrent of emotion burst out of him, he laughed, he was menacing—he lived every part. It was a dazzling display of virtuosity.

Suddenly, he interrupted himself: "No, no . . . this is wrong . . . she wouldn't say this . . . that's not her character . . ." but three pages later he would furiously hit his forehead with the open of his hand: "Oh, what a fool I am . . . what an utter fool . . . of *course* it's right . . . of yes . . . it's *so* right . . . that's *exactly* how she would talk." He read through the whole script, searching, dissecting it, and making it a thing of beauty. When the train stopped at Albuquerque, he showed me a telegram he was sending off to Charles Koerner, then the head of RKO. It was full of gratitude and very humble. "What a tremendous challenge for a tired old ham," it ended. For the next few days, he talked of nothing but the film.

"I will never become a great actor," I thought after having witnessed Laughton. "I can't get so completely absorbed in a play . . . I cannot breathe and think theater or films with such fire and fervor . . . I am probably not living an actor's life." It was a sad realization.

The day after we arrived in Hollywood, I had lunch with Jean Renoir, our director, and Dudley Nichols, who had written the screenplay. I told them about my trip with Laughton, about his first reaction to the script and how terribly impressed I was. They both looked at me and laughed. "What are you talking about?" said Dudley Nichols. "Charlie has had the script for the last eight weeks!"

Jean Renoir has a wonderful sly way with actors. After a scene has been shot, he is full of praise, embraces you, makes you believe that you have surpassed yourself, that the scene was flawless and inspired, that you cannot possibly fail to win the Academy Award this time. Then he will say:

"Shust for de luck—we shoot it again!"

I was doing a scene with George Sanders. I had one of my off days. I knew I was doing it badly, but Renoir was nice and patient. We kept on rehearsing and rehearsing—the cameraman growled, "O.K., boy, cut your arcs," and the big lights went out. I saw that the electricians in the rafters were lighting cigarettes, getting out the racing sheets, and settling down to what promised to be a lengthy recess. Just then Laughton walked on the set. I excused myself and went over to him. "Charlie, read that scene for me!" His face lit up; he grinned like an amused Cheshire cat: "What's the matter . . . ? NO talent?" "None whatsoever—*today!*" I said. "Please read!" He did. I went back on the set, and we shot the scene in one take. Renoir didn't even ask to repeat it "Shust for de luck."

When I thanked Laughton, he said, "Of course, my boy, there are several ways of doing it," and he read it three more times . . . every time with a different attack, a different interpretation, and a new characterization. I was ready to turn in my Actors Equity card.

We had a long and difficult scene coming up. It was played in jail, in the cell where Laughton was being held and where I, as the Nazi officer, tried to make the philosophy of the Third Reich palatable to him. Charlie asked me if I would come to his home and run over the lines with him a few times. Of course, I jumped at the chance.

I arrived at his lovely, elaborate house in Pacific Palisades. A butler led me into a beautifully proportioned room which looked out on a terrace in the garden, with the ocean in the background. On one wall hung *The Judgment of Paris,* one of the great Renoir paintings, an outstanding Braque, some very good African sculpture, and over the mantel was a charming little Rousseau. It was just a hand, delicately holding one rose. We began to read the scene. At first, he read it haltingly, as if the words didn't make sense; at the second reading, it got more fluent. It took shape, and with great delight I began to realize that I was given a performance of "AN ACTOR CREATES!" Charlie, of course, had forgotten that he had already played the scene brilliantly for me on the train.

When we shot the scene, and the time for my close-up came, he insisted (although he was not in the picture and just sitting next to the camera, giving me the cues) that a light should shine in his face. "Walter *has* to be able to see my eyes," he declared.

It was a narrow set and a light in his eyes would also shine into the lens of the camera; so they had to dismantle the set and build a partition from which his eyes were lit.

I began my close-up, which was practically a monologue, and saw that Laughton's eyes were filling with tears; he pressed a hand against his mouth as if to prevent himself from crying out. His face became contorted, and when the scene was over, he collapsed in his chair with a groan. I rushed over to him. "Charlie, are you all right?" I thought he was in pain. He looked up—worn, exhausted, spent—and whispered: "Oh, my dear boy, it's so difficult to keep it simple!"

I adore him.

Once a year, opera comes to Los Angeles. It stays six short weeks and can be heard and seen at the Shrine Auditorium. That huge edifice was erected in all its spectacular ugliness with the intention of housing Shriners' conventions and pageants. It is eminently unsuited for playing opera. The musicians' pit is practically level with the stage and the orchestra floor, the acoustics are abominable and are not helped by a system of amplification that manages to make even the loveliest voices sound coarse and shrill. It has more dead spots where nothing can be heard than any other auditorium I know: with the memorable exception of an ice-hockey arena in Toronto, where the Metropolitan Opera Company used to bed down for five days on its yearly spring tour.

But Los Angeles is a cultural desert. With the exception of the summer concerts at the Hollywood Bowl, a few operettas at the Philharmonic, and an occasional road company of a Broadway play, the town definitely does not lead the life of a metropolis of seven million people. Thus, the small minority who remain unthrilled by watching the gala première of *Grandson of Rin Tin Tin* at Cathay Circle, complete with klieg lights, screaming mobs in the bleachers, and full television coverage, and who do not enjoy crowding into a noisy night club and watch the movie stars get drunk and fight—for these few hardy nonconformists, opera, *even* at the Shrine, is a big event.

So my best girl and I regularly braved the freeway traffic and drove downtown for every performance—she wearing orchids in her hair and looking so lovely, and I, wearing a spotless tuxedo and looking so distinguished. I had been wooing and serenading her for several months and had observed that the name Johanna did not lend itself to the billing, cooing, and purring of my lovesick babble. The name sounded official, formal, and statuesque, so I changed it to "Kaasi," a derivative from the Dutch *Kaaskop* (cheese head), and by that *nom d'amour* she is now known. We were completely attuned to each other, were able to talk shorthand, just a word or a look brought instant rapport. We even heard music, as it were, with the same pair of ears. A singer's slightest deviation from pitch made us wince in unison, and a melodic phrase, especially well sung and beautiful, made us nudge each other and smile—in unison. We were, in the words of Mr. Oblo, "constantly elated."

On "that night," as we refer to it now, the opera was *La Traviata*. Bidu Sayao sang, and Jan Peerce, both at the top of their form—it was a joy. After the performance, we drove back together in silence. We had to stop for a red light. "You know, of course, that you will marry me," I said, and then the lights changed. She didn't answer me, didn't even say: "Oh . . . ?" So I regarded the matter as closed.

The following day she told Mme. Schwarz: "Walter asked me to marry him!" She was probing for comment! Mme. Schwarz laughed her most silvery operatic laugh. "*Walter*, wanting to get married—ha ha ha ha. You just try him and say 'YES' and you will see how fast he'll run and disappear." So she tried me and said "YES." That was twenty blissful years ago. Dear Vera Schwarz is still surprised.

In 1938, I costarred with Vera Zorina and Vivienne Segal in the Rodgers & Hart musical *I Married an Angel*. It was a solid smash hit, and naturally I couldn't leave for my yearly summer vacation with my parents. So they came to America instead and visited me.

When the S.S. *Europa* steamed up the harbor of New

York, I climbed aboard at Quarantine—a reporter from the *Herald Tribune* had taken me along on the tender. Papa embraced me and with great urgency whispered in my ear: "Be very careful what you say." He refused to talk to newspaper people, or give interviews, for fear of being asked questions about the Nazis, and inadvertently saying something that might prove fatal when they returned to Germany. Even after we had landed and were in the privacy of his hotel room, every time he spoke of conditions in Germany and Austria, he first looked left, right, and behind him to make sure no one was watching or eavesdropping. It had become their habit to be on constant guard. And to whisper. Mama asked me again and again if I was absolutely certain that there were no microphones hidden in the room. It took them a few days to get used to the idea that over here they could say what they wanted.

In the year 1938, Austria had already been annexed by Adolf Hitler's brown tyranny, and foreign-currency restrictions were rigid. As long as Papa could pay in Austrian or German money, he was a wealthy man; and they arrived occupying the presidential suite on the S.S. *Europa.*

But they could take no money out of the country, and when they stepped off the boat they had only eight dollars between them. In Europe, when we traveled, Papa always paid for me. He would have considered it ridiculous had I tried to pick up a check in a restaurant or pay for theater tickets or a cab. And it was always terribly hard to buy him a present: he wanted nothing, because he had everything.

Several times I presented him with personalized stationery, but it just made him sad. "Look, my boy," he would say, and open a closet that was filled to the brim with envelopes and writing paper stolen from all over the world. "I don't NEED any—it's just a terrible waste of your money to give me something I don't NEED."

Papa had always been an avid collector of hotel stationery.

So avid, in fact, that he *never* bought any of his own; anyway, not until the advent of air-mail service dictated economy by the use of onionskin paper. In 1928, fourteen years after he had left the United States, some of his mail to me still bore the Hotel Ansonia letterhead.

So now, for the first time in my life, I had a chance to spoil them. I rented a lovely suite of rooms for them at the Beekman Hotel. But both Papa and Mama were terribly concerned that their "child" would spend too much money on them, that they might be a financial burden to me, and they insisted on knowing how much everything cost. So the manager of the hotel and I put our heads together, and two sets of weekly bills were made up—the true amount, which I paid without Papa ever seeing it, and an elaborately falsified statement, where every item was listed at half of its real price and where the words "Summer Rate" and "Professional Discount" put the seal of credibility on our big lie. Whenever I took them to an expensive restaurant, I telephoned ahead, asking that no bill of fare be brought to the table and that I would be presented with only a reasonably small bill. The true bill was to be mailed to my home.

I very much doubt if Papa was really fooled by my deceptions. He was far too smart for that, but he graciously played along with my little game. Mama, of course, who was completely naïve in money matters, who never had her own bank account, and wouldn't have known how to write out a check, believed it all and often marveled how inexpensive New York was.

At our home in Europe, Mama was given, as was then the custom, every month a certain amount of money to run the house. Meticulously she wrote down every item that was spent, and if at the end of the month there was a shortage of eleven pennies, she was terribly upset and troubled. "Stop brooding," Papa said, "and put it down to miscellaneous." The household money was kept in her linen closet, in a little metal box that was always locked. Sometimes she mislaid the key, and frantic searches were launched in which the whole family, with the notable exception of Papa, had to join. One day I offered to open the lock with a hairpin; she stared at me in blank horror, as if she had spawned a professional safecracker. Three times a year, I had to steal the key from her and bring it, with the box, to Papa. That always happened a few weeks before his birthday, his nameday, and before Christmas. He would then put extra money in the box so she could buy him a present without having to ask for additional funds. She never caught on, the dear, dear soul, and always wondered in great puzzlement how it was possible that she had so much left over. She was completely without guile and childlike in her trust.

I remember that one day, many, many years back in Vienna, she came home very excited and raved about a beautiful rococo vitrine she had seen in the window of an antique shop. It was French, around 1740, an exquisite piece in perfect condition. "Just for curiosity's sake, I asked the price, but that was outrageous, far too expensive, but it *was* a lovely piece."

"*Liebling*," Papa said, "if you like it that much, why don't you buy it?"

"I wouldn't think of spending so much of your hard-earned money."

A few days later she went around the house humming. Whenever she was sad or depressed, she hummed, and she got real angry when Papa said, "*Liebling*, don't sing—you don't know how." Later, when I was older, and I said it to her, she always snapped at me. She kept on humming until I discovered the cause. She had passed the antique shop again. The rococo vitrine was no longer in the window. She inquired and was told that it had been sold.

Christmas in our house was Papa's personal domain. He was in charge of all arrangements except the trimming of the tree, and that he supervised with sage admonitions and lots of criticism while sitting in a comfortable chair.

One Christmas, it was around December 22, friends sent us a large potted palm. Papa happened to be at the front door when it arrived. He quickly took away the card that accompanied it and instructed the messenger to deliver it to our lawyer. "That's one Christmas gift less we have to send," was his happy comment. But on the twenty-fourth in the evening, at seven o'clock, the potted palm was back. It had gone through seven hands. Each one had passed it on. He had to keep it, and it was referred to as "the clearing present."

We always celebrated Christmas on the twenty-fourth in the evening in the music salon just after it got dark. Each one had his traditional place, on which his presents were displayed. Mama arranged them all, except her own. Papa's gifts were heaped on the piano and then covered with a sheet, then Mama left the room, Papa entered, and he was put on his honor not to peek. He then arranged her presents, lit the candles on the tree; we all waited outside, and then he rang a small silver bell and called out: "*Das Christkind ist hier*" (The Christ Child is here). We all marched in, Mama took the sheet off the piano, the maids came in and got their gifts, and Christmas began. But on one particular Christmas I recall, when we marched in, there in the middle of the room stood—the rococo vitrine. Mama just stared at it, unbelieving. "But they said it was sold!" she kept repeating. Papa had bought it the day after Mama had talked about it.

After Papa had said farewell to the opera stage, he began a big new career as a comedian in German and Austrian movies. Doing films was like a vacation for him after the constant responsibility and concern about being in good voice. If a scene wasn't good the first time, one just did it over until it was right—no pressure and no stage fright.

While he was at the Met, he lived in constant fear of getting hoarse; the New York climate was his sworn enemy. So he barely went out, and he only saw the Ansonia Hotel, the inside of our carriage, and the Metropolitan Opera. And practically nothing of New York. It became my happy lot to show him *Our Town*. The first thing he wanted to revisit was the Metropolitan Opera. It was summer and the Met was closed. But Constance Hope, a dear friend of mine, who was then director of public relations for the Met, managed to have it opened for us, to have the curtain raised, and all the lights put on—and there he stood again, on that grand old stage, and looked out into one of the most glorious opera houses of the world. He pointed out the box Mama and we children had always occupied. He reminisced about the great Geraldine Farrar, her lovely voice, and breath-taking beauty. She had sung in Humperdinck's *Die Koenigskinder*, and when she took her curtain call, she carried a live goose under her arm. The goose screamed, and the people found it lovely. Whereupon Papa informed her that at his next *Lohengrin* performance, he would take the swan with him for a curtain call. "All right, go ahead," she laughed, "but you can pinch your swan all you want—he still won't scream—he is stuffed." When I played Zsupan in *The Gypsy Baron* during the 1959–60 Metropolitan Opera season, I also took livestock with me on my curtain call—Cyril, my suckling pig, and he squealed *without* being pinched.

Papa showed me where his dressing room had been, where Arturo Toscanini had banged his head against the wall because Papa had "swallowed a quarter note." He talked of Gatti-Casazza, Gustav Mahler. He told Constance how he had sung the duke in *Rigoletto* with a tiny little Gilda who didn't weigh more than a hundred ten pounds, and how silly it always struck him that Rigoletto was supposed to believe that Papa's six foot seven, three-hundred-pound body would be in that bag. How he and Emmy Destinn, after a performance of Mozart's *Magic Flute,* had gone to Ringling Brothers to christen a newly born camel, and how she had thrown him a curve and named the camel Leo. He then promised her that he would see to it that the next rhinoceros born in captivity would be named Emmy.

He recalled how Frances Alda, during a performance of Verdi's *Otello,* had suffered an acute attack of appendicitis, and how the publicity man for the Met had given out the story that Mr. Slezak, in his brutal, bestial impersonation of the moor of Venice, had hurled her to the floor with such force that her appendix broke, loudly enough to be heard as far back as the fourteenth row. And after his next performance the lead of the review read: "Giant Czech Appendix Breaker Wins Audience." He talked of Scotti and Amato, who sang Iago with him, of Tetrazzini, Mme. Nordica, and wonderful Mme. Schumann-Heink.

Papa told her about a *Lohengrin* performance. It was just before his first entrance. He was ready to step into the boat, which, drawn by a swan, was to take him on-stage. Somehow the stagehand on the other side got his signals mixed, started pulling, and the swan left without Papa. He quietly turned around and said: "What time's the next swan?"

That story has since become a classic in operatic lore. Papa continued:

"One of the baritones at the Vienna Opera always wore large cotton plugs in his ears to ward off colds. He walked around with them on the street, everywhere he went; at rehearsals he took them off, laid them on the piano, sang; and when he left he replaced them. One night this man was singing Jokanaan in Richard Strauss's *Salome.* Just before the performance I managed to sneak, unobserved, into the prop room. And when, on a silver platter, the papier-mâché head of Jokanaan emerged from the well, it wore in each ear two-inch-long gleaming white earplugs. Poor Salome and everyone, even the orchestra, laughed so hard they all but had to ring down the curtain."

"I was never found out!" he added proudly.

He told her about a performance of Gluck's *Armide* at the Met. The opera was over and he saw a dignified old gentleman with a long flowing white beard standing around. With an iron grip he grabbed him and pulled him out with him in front of the curtain to take a bow. There he pointed to the bewildered old gent and bowed deeply. Two reporters rushed backstage to Papa's dressing room. "That was Mr. Willibald Gluck, the composer!" Papa said reverently. "He told me that never in his life has he heard his opera sung so magnificently as I have sung it tonight." The following day two large metropolitan newspapers, who apparently weren't aware of the fact that Christoph Willibald von Gluck had died in 1787, printed the story. Papa was fined one hundred dollars by the Met. He put a black veil over his head and went to the office of Otto H. Kahn, the Maecenas of the opera. He got his hundred dollars back.

Papa then showed us in which part of the gallery that nefarious blackmailing outfit, the "claque" was seated when they arranged "spontaneous ovations." (Today they are still in the same seats, left and right corner in the upper gallery.)

In those days *everybody* at the Met had to pay the claque, because the ones who didn't would be hissed at and insulted with catcalls and bronx cheers, or a sudden outburst of frenetic applause would start just *before* an aria was finished, while the last floating pianissimo was still in the air, which, of course, spoiled the whole effect. Some of the singers, mostly the Italian contingent, not only would pay to have *themselves* applauded and cheered, they would also pay to have their rivals booed. And it would then be up to the "rival" to make a better financial arrangement with the chief of the claque.

Then we visited Carnegie Hall and tried to find the old Aeolian Hall, that once famous concert auditorium; but it had long since been torn down.

We did the entire tourist bit—from Grant's tomb to the top of the Empire State, from Chinatown to Lüchow's. They saw all the shows on Broadway, all the good movies, and every weekend we went to my country place, where I enriched their lives by introducing them to barbecuing, a form of cookery not well known in the old country.

I begged them to stay in America and not return to Germany, but Papa was sure that in such a case the Nazis would confiscate all his property and put my eighty-eight-year-old grandmother and my sister in a concentration camp. "Over here, I am a pauper," he explained. "I am sixty-five years old, too old to start anew in a strange country—in a strange language."

They were so happy and carefree here, but the moment they boarded the *Bremen* for the return trip, they were taut and reserved and began to whisper again.

Came the summer of 1939 and I sailed for Europe. In Hamburg, when I disembarked and went through German customs, a black-uniformed S.S. man checked my passport. He slowly raised his head and stared at me, took out a small notebook, wrote down my name, returned the passport and said: "Walter Slezak—an American citizen? That's interesting!" I felt extremely uncomfortable.

In Papa's study in Tegernsee I noticed that our telephone was placed on a felt pad and was covered by a heavily quilted tea cozy. Papa whispered, "A repairman arrived, claimed that there was something wrong with the phone! There is now a microphone concealed, so we just cover it and speak softly."

Everybody who had friends or relatives living outside Germany was suspect, was watched and spied on. A few days later on the street, I met a fellow I had known since childhood. We had grown up together as boys. His father was now the mayor of Tegernsee. "What a coincidence," he exclaimed. "Only last night Father was talking about you. There was an inquiry why you are not a party member and why you are not registered for the draft!"

"Because I am an American citizen, you silly baboon," I replied.

"Oh, we know *that!* But Father said that we don't recognize it. You were born in Austria, and Austria is now a part of the greater German Reich. As far as we are concerned, you are a German citizen." I ran to the next telephone booth and called the American Consul in Munich, who confirmed what Max had told me.

"If they take away your passport, we will most certainly register a strong protest," he explained. "*But,*" he added, "I very much doubt if the United States will go to war over you."

I rushed home, alerted our chauffeur, and three hours later I was in Switzerland. Bright and early the following day four brown-clad storm troopers marched into our house and demanded to see me. "Oh, but he isn't here any longer." Papa's voice was dripping with regret. "He left last night—for America!"

With four more weeks of vacation time left, I stayed in Switzerland. About a year earlier I had started to get pudgy and decided to do something about it right then. I checked into a reducing sanatorium in Degersheim, a village near St. Gall; and there I began the initial battle in my war against overexpansion, a war that I have now been waging in slow but constant retreat for over twenty-three years.

Successful attacks against the bulge of solid flab gave way to depressing defeats, followed by a "What the hell, let it spread" attitude. Up and down the bathroom scale this war still rages on. Being a man who honestly confides everything, including his true weight, to his diary, and being interested in statistics, I figured out that from August of 1939 to the day this book went to press, I have gained AND lost a total sum of 1273 pounds. Every diet that was ever invented I tried. For a while I ate nothing but bananas and skim milk until I felt like a suckling chimpanzee—I fed on stale black bread and red wine; and was pleasantly drunk for weeks. I shoveled carbohydrates and vitamin-enriched high proteins into me, all sorts of fruit, pot cheeses in every form (except creamed), at the Rye Krisp plant my name is mentioned in reverence and manufacturers of dietetic foods genuflect when they see my picture in the papers. Hefty masseurs have lost pounds and pounds while working over me; I have owned regular torture chambers, with electric steam cabinets, bar bells, rowing machines, vibrating belts; I have worn out hundreds of pairs of shoes taking long walks. I must have walked at least twice around the globe. In one reducing asylum I was chased, stark naked, at six in the morning around a meadow that was still wet with dew, and had to perform acrobatic calisthenics that would have made me a star in every tribal dance in Africa. After that, I was set into five inches of ice-cold water and had to slap it over my body. I was fed nothing but water and sand—to cleanse my system. After three days of that I had such halitosis I was ashamed to exhale. I have been pricked with injections of reducing fluids until my fanny looked like a two-hump pincushion. I have taken pills so profitable to the druggists that two of them have retired to Florida. I have eaten disgusting bulk to spoil my appetite—wafers, grain, meal—all stuff that was to be taken with water and then would swell inside me and kill the pangs of appetite.

When hungry, I am mean, evil, and nasty.

When well fed and sated, I am adorable, lovable, and saintlike in my disposition.

I am still seventy-five pounds overweight.

My mother had always had premonitions. In 1910 we attended a circus performance in Chicago in a box that was level with the arena. Mama suddenly grabbed us children, rushed out, and frantically called for Papa to follow her. Two minutes later the elephants stampeded, trampled our box, and four people were killed.

Once, while playing a scene in a film in Berlin, some draperies caught fire and the whole set went up in flames. I was only slightly burned and received immediate first aid. While I was still being bandaged, Mama was on the phone. She was in Amsterdam, where Papa was singing at the Concertgebouw; she had called my home and been told that I was in the studio. "Walter, *mein Bub,*" she cried. "Are you all right? I feel that you are in danger. I feel fire!"

So when she called me from Tegernsee and begged me—in the guarded language they had to use on the phone—to "return to America as soon as possible," I quickly made my boat reservations.

Papa somehow wangled permission for them to drive to Switzerland, and we spent two days together. They were convinced that war was imminent. They had observed great troop movements. It was difficult to buy gasoline, and the "patriotic attitude" was the same as in 1914.

It was a sad parting. That day I wrote in my diary: "Will I ever see them again?" In 1946, after both of them had passed away, I leafed through Papa's diary, and on that day he had written: "Sad good-by with Walter; I am afraid we will never see him again."

On my way to Paris, and from there on to Cherbourg, I spent one night in Zurich. It was the time of the *"Landi,"* the Swiss Exposition, and the town was full. I had to stay at a small hotel nobody ever heard of. My train for Paris was leaving early in the morning. I left a call, but the "staff" of that hotel never woke me up. I was furious, and when I rushed down to pay my bill the owner of the hotel, a Mr. Ruessli, charged me twice the amount that had been agreed with the room clerk the night before. As I didn't want to miss my train, I paid, put my luggage into a taxi, but returned and, boiling with rage, told Mr. Ruessli what I thought of him. I called him a *Betrueger* (cheat), *Dieb* (thief), *Verbrecher* (criminal), *Gauner* (crook), and *Wegelagerer* (highway robber). Our encounter ended with a right uppercut to the chin that sent him sprawling across the lobby. At the railway station and in the train I was very much afraid that he would have me arrested for assault, and I breathed a sigh of relief when we crossed the French border. But as I got off the train in Paris, I missed my brand-new, beautiful, very expensive, silk-lined, yellow camel's-hair coat, which I had purchased only a week earlier. And with a sinking heart I remembered where I had left it. On a hanger, behind the door of my room in Mr. Ruessli's hotel. I called there and BEGGED that they should PLEASE be so KIND and mail it to me, EXPRESS, to the Hôtel Rond-Point des Champs-Elysées in Paris, as my boat for America was leaving in two days. The two days passed and, coatless, I stepped into a taxi that was to take me to the boat train for Cherbourg. And as the taxi began to move, a bellboy ran up, handing me a large cardboard box. It was addressed to me, and in the upper left-hand corner I read: "Sender: Mr. Ruessli, Betrueger, Dieb, Verbrecher, Gauner, Wegelagerer!"

I wrote him a letter of thanks, said I was sorry for the right uppercut, and resolved that someday I would open a secret-number bank account in Switzerland.

We were shooting the film *Lifeboat.* In it I played the captain of the rammed German submarine who is picked up by the survivors of the steamer he has torpedoed. To give my appearance an extra coat of deceptive harmlessness, Alfred

Hitchcock thought it would be a nice idea if I had curly hair, and I was given a permanent wave. But somehow it didn't take and I looked like a sick caracul lamb. So every morning at seven I had to report to the hairdressing department to be manhandled by a curling iron. There the glamorous ladies of the cinema sat in their styling chairs in one long row and were being made alluring for the day's shooting. Like them I was covered with a shampoo cape and somehow they forgot that an outsider was sitting in their midst. My vocabulary of the unprintable grew with every session. The most intimate incidents, the habits and the practices of their most private lives were most indiscreetly confided and discussed. I doubt if there exists a man's locker room that could match their colorful conversation. It was always a letdown to have to leave this happy little group, go on the sound stage, and just listen to Tallulah Bankhead.

During the filming of *Lifeboat* Kaasi and I got married. We had rented a very nice house with a large garden in Beverly Hills. As I was working every day at the studio, all arrangements for the reception, catering, liquor, and champagne, kitchen help, waiters, and music, were taken care of by my agent. Half an hour before the guests arrived, in walked a cello, a violin, and a harp! They were being lugged by three ladies dressed in flowing robes of blue, pink, and yellow chiffon. What I first believed to be halloween masks turned out to be their true faces. Now I was firmly convinced that under their startling exterior there flowered three lovely souls, but I wasn't sure that my guests would share my belief, so I led them to the far end of the garden into a bougainvillaea-covered pergola. They were so far away that only occasionally, when the wind changed directions, a few snatches of music wafted our way. The rest of the time was like silent pictures: motion, but no sound.

In beautiful contrast to them was Thelma, the girl in charge of coats and hats. She was a stunning creature. My aunt, an elderly vigilante, functioning as store detective, called me aside and, quivering with happy outrage, told me that each male guest, with his claim check, was handed a small card on which were neatly printed Thelma's name and address and the touching message: "LONELY?? CALL ME!" Auntie also managed, by flying tackle, to stop a waiter from carrying a case of champagne to his car. Not content with this act of bravery, she forced the poor man to open the trunk of his automobile and return to the pantry two more cases he had already stowed away. She was also able to recount exactly how many sandwiches and how much champagne each guest had consumed. We had invited around seventy-five people, but a hundred fifty showed up, crowding around the buffet and the bar and using my bathroom. At five o'clock my little bride and I left for Santa Barbara. I had to be back on the set the next day.

Working with Alfred Hitchcock was a great experience. He knows precisely what he wants to say and show in each shot. He pinpoints the essence, the core. During the scene when I amputate William Bendix's leg, he kept the camera outside the boat, behind the helmsman's back. I asked him why, because usually operations are shown in close-ups, with the action of scalpel, sutures, and the masked faces of the doctors and the nurses' frightened eyes showing. "All that has been done," he explained. "I want to show the hazard of doing an operation in an open boat, against the background of an oncoming storm."

The young actress who played the nurse had trouble with a very emotional scene. Hitchcock waited for her to get into the mood, then he said: "Look, child, we haven't got that much time! First of all you will drop your voice about three notes. You will then take one long deep breath and begin talking. At that and that line your breath will give out—but you *will keep on talking,* even if I can't hear a word of what you are saying! Let's shoot!"

They did the scene in one take. At the exact line where Hitchcock had predicted, her breath gave out, but she kept on mouthing the words. And suddenly you had a feeling, that there was a girl who was completely spent; her parched lips, after forty-two days on the open sea, quivered and trembled. She didn't have the strength to make them heard, but you understood everything she said. Hitch knows more about the mechanics and the physical technique of acting than any man I know.

Six months after we had been married we read in Hedda Hopper's column that we were expecting a baby. We didn't know anything about it and were very much surprised; even more so when it turned out to be true.

We wanted the child to be born in our own home, so we decided to buy. We had fifteen thousand dollars in a savings account and went house-hunting. Now most Hollywood personalities would have used that money as down payment on a sixty-five-thousand-dollar house, but not my frugal, clever little Dutch wife. "We will buy a house for fifteen thousand, or LESS," she decreed. That ruled out fancy Beverly Hills; we found a large comfortable home (rugs, icebox, and stove included) in what the real estate agent described as a choice location. As long as the war lasted it certainly was just that: half a block away from Sunset Boulevard, supermarkets, drycleaners, and Schwab's drugstore just a stone's throw away. Every homeowner in Los Angeles always brags that on a clear day he can see Catalina Island; well, we could see Greenblatt's delicatessen ANY day, even when it was foggy. Gasoline rationing didn't affect us, the bus stopped at the corner, and the maid didn't have to be picked up and driven back on her day off.

Having never been a father before, at least not knowingly, I bought volumes and volumes of books on prenatal and postnatal care; I studied medical textbooks on child delivery. In my dramatic fancies I considered the possibility that we might be snowbound in a lonely mountain cabin, stalled in a car in the Mojave Desert, or trapped in an elevator with power failure. I wanted to be prepared. I drove the road from our house to the Hollywood Presbyterian Hospital over and over; stopwatch in hand, I clocked every trial run in light and in heavy traffic. Whenever I didn't work at the studio I accompanied my wife to the doctor's office and drove him crazy with questions and admonitions. I bought myself a stethoscope and listened to the heartbeat of my child. Ten weeks before the baby was due, my wife's bag for the hospital was ready and packed; accessible in the middle of the hall, where everybody tripped over it.

D-Day arrived, and at 6 A.M. we drove to the hospital. The night nurse refused to admit my wife until I made a large deposit, and she didn't want to accept my check. I never was overly fond of nurses, but for this one I exploded in glaring hatred. She was saved from being mutilated by the arrival of our obstetrician, who graciously went bail for me. I was permitted to accompany my sweet little balloon girl up to the door of the labor room. Then I had to leave. But before I left, out of another labor room, I heard an ear-piercing scream. I turned ashen. "What's happening in there?" I asked a strolling nurse. "Oh, she's coming along nicely," was her airy reply.

I was then shooting the film *The Spanish Main* and on that day I was supposed to check in at 8 A.M. for a scene with three hundred fifty extras. I called Charlie Koerner, of RKO studios, at his home and begged him for permission to come in later. "Hell no," he said gruffly. "Your place is with your wife. Stay at the hospital and call me when the baby has arrived." He paid off three hundred fifty extras and closed the set. Charlie was one of the last princes. They don't come like that any more.

I then began my vigil in the "fathers' room." The atmosphere was oppressive and claustrophobic. One poor guy had been waiting there for thirty-two hours. He was unshaved, chain-smoked, and babbled incoherently about how much he disliked his father-in-law. I figured him as the victim of a shotgun wedding. A grandmother sat with us, and every time a nurse stuck her head in the door and announced: "Congratulations, Mr. So-and-So, you have a baby boy," she cried and said: "Just imagine—another little rascal born." After the sixth little rascal I was ready to strangle her. I became more on edge as the hours dragged on; every time I asked how my wife was doing, I got the answer: "She is doing it according to the book." After seventeen hours of stewing in uncertainty and of imagining horrible tragedies, I began to crack up. I marched out into the hall, grabbed the first nurse that ambled by, forcibly leaned her against the wall, and hissed: "Now you listen to me! You are going in there and tell them that I want to find out what's going on. For all I know my wife might be dead and somebody forgot to tell me about it. If I don't get a full report within two minutes, I am going in there myself! And never mind that sign: NO ADMISSION!" I propelled her on her way! She came back almost immediately and assured me that my wife was coming along nicely and was doing it according to the book.

They must have flashed a warning to the hospital staff that there was a madman on the loose who might run amok any minute, because a nice elderly nurse approached me as if I were a snarling beast that had to be soothed. She took me to the diet kitchen and started to make coffee for me. While we waited for the water to boil, she tried to calm me down by telling me how much she liked my performance in *Lifeboat*. The film had just been released and she proceeded to tell me the story.

"Then the survivors in the boat hear a voice calling way out in the sea, and through the fog they see a man swimming toward the boat. He holds a woman in his arm and the woman is clutching her newborn baby." Then she leaned toward me and whispered: "The baby is dead, but the mother doesn't know it! After the baby is handed into the boat, they all see that it's dead, but the mother doesn't know it." She kept on talking and describing the dead baby—I sat there, stunned, afraid to breathe. All I could think was: She is trying to tell me something, she is trying to prepare me. I was cold with the sweat of fear. She continued with her narration, and when she came to the sequence of the big storm, I carefully interrupted: "I KNOW the story, you see—I made the picture."

"So you did!" she answered pleasantly, and handed me a cup of coffee. Just then I heard hurried footsteps on the linoleum of the hall. "Mr. Slezak, oh, Mr. Slezak . . ." I stumbled to the door. A tall nurse, her face mask pulled down over her chin, beamed at me: "Congratulations, you have a little baby girl." I burst into tears. The tall nurse put her arms around me and led me into the delivery room. I embraced my beloved and was introduced to Ingrid Elisabeth Maria Slezak, eleven minutes old.

On that day, six thousand miles away, in Tegernsee, my father wrote in his diary: "Freezing cold, no more coal, stayed in bed fully dressed. Tremendous air attack on Munich, can hear explosions, sky fiery red. 231 days since my dearest dearest one left me, since the light of my life went out."

Good, gentle, tender Mama had died nearly eight months earlier. The one act of grace they had been praying for all their lives, to leave together, had not been granted. Papa's Red Cross message took four months to reach me. He was a completely broken man, a lost soul. A few months later the war was over; his letters were heartrending; he had only one wish: to say good-by to me and to follow his beloved.

All my attempts to visit him were blocked because my sister had been on friendly terms with Adolf Hitler, a fact that was well known in Germany and of which the American Army of Occupation was also aware. With the help of Bob Hope, who got in touch with the commander for the Bavarian sector, we managed to have Papa's home declared off limits and he was never bothered by billets or by the carpetbagger civilians who followed the army and often liberated the entire contents of private homes.

Once, during the course of the war, Papa had managed to have a letter smuggled to Switzerland from where it was mailed to me in Hollywood.

"Our glorious Fuehrer," he wrote with sneering sarcasm, "has so wisely planned our economy that we are existing on a completely fat-free diet. Buying new clothes is considered detrimental to the war effort and an act of treason, so I have decided, ardent patriot that I am, to walk about in my old ones. Every time I appear on the streets I present a picture of mirth and hilarity, because I have, so far, lost 115 pounds. The happiest creatures in Germany are the singing birds, because there are no more cats left. The beer is so thin that I wrote a letter to the brewmaster of Löwenbrau beer. 'Please send me the color, I have the water.'"

So, after the hostilities had ended, my first job was to feed him. At random I collected names of soldiers who were stationed in and around Munich, sent them quantities of the regulation five-pound packages and begged them to pass them on to Papa. Many, many of them obliged, and out of 958 packages we sent Papa received 457.

On June 1, 1946, he closed his eyes for the last time and joined his beloved Elsa.

Finally, two months too late, I received permission to fly to Germany. It was a sad homecoming. Mama, my grandmother, Papa, all gone; the house empty, the grounds neglected, every tree, including the ones Papa had planted thirty-five years earlier, cut down during the war by Nazi work brigades. Hostility from the few old friends that were left; they treated me with sarcastic mock deference as one of the victors.

I couldn't wait to get back to my wife, my little Ingrid, and to tiny Erika, who had been born three weeks before I left. But my return trip was stopped in Paris, where I was hopelessly stuck for a full week. All TWA planes were grounded, every boat sailing to America was overbooked, and no chance to get a ride on a military transport. I tried a roundabout way: I bribed my way on a plane that was leaving Paris, via Lisbon, Dakar, to Recife, Brazil.

But, to travel in Brazil, one needs a Brazilian visa, and, to get a Brazilian visa, one needs a health certificate; and that health certificate has to be certified by a Brazilian doctor who is accredited with the Brazilian Consulate. And they had only one such man, a Dr. De Lima. And he saw patients only on Friday from 2 to 4 P.M. The rest of the time he was out of town. And my plane was to leave on Wednesday.

All this was told to me, very matter of factly, by the airline official who had pocketed my bribe money, and with a "*je regrette infiniment*" he turned away from me and went out to lunch.

In 1946 in Paris, to be able to conclude two telephone conversations and find a taxi constituted a full day's work. But somehow I got to the Brazilian Consulate, where I learned Dr. De Lima's home address and also picked up the information that Brazil requires passport photos of a special size, not common in other countries, and I was given the address of a Brazilian photographer who, I was assured, was the only man in Paris who could take the kind of photograph the consulate would accept as perfect.

My first trip was to the residence of Dr. De Lima. I rang the doorbell and a man in shirt sleeves opened the door and said gruffly: "The doctor is not in!" But on a hunch born out of desperation I put my foot in the door and said: "Dear Doctor, we know each other; don't you remember, we have met!"

"We have?" He sounded doubtful but asked me in. In his salon hung a large portrait of a lady whom I recognized immediately. With reverence I pointed to her and said: "Ah, *la grande Mistinguett!* We met through *her!*"

"Oh, that's possible," he said, relenting. "I meet so many people at Mother's." And he apologized for not remembering me. I glanced over my left shoulder and blew a kiss to my guardian angel, who, I was firmly convinced, was standing there. Ten minutes later I left, clutching written and certified proof that I had been inoculated against every known and unknown disease and had been found a fit specimen to journey to and through Brazil. The dear doctor even refused to accept money "From one of Mother's old friends." A rare occurrence among doctors anywhere and an unheard-of thing in France.

My next stop was at the Brazilian photographer's, where I posed for my passport photos. "They will be ready in three days," he assured me. But for five times the regular fee, plus "*quelque chose pour l'encouragement,*" I took them with me in half an hour.

After America had entered the war in December 1941 all postal service with Germany and Austria was stopped. But Papa had faithfully kept on writing to me, a ten-page letter nearly every week. They were never mailed and I found them, neatly bundled, sealed and addressed to me. Though Papa had attended school only until he was fourteen years old, he had made himself a highly literate man and was a wonderful writer. He had that rare talent to be able to write the way he talked. His first book, a humorous autobiography, was published in 1924. He called it *Meine saemtlichen Werke* (My Entire Works) and promised that he would never write another book. But its success was so spectacular (it sold over six hundred thousand copies) that he did write another one *Der Wortbruch* (The Breach of Promise) and after that a third, *Der Rueckfall* (The Relapse).

They are still on the best-seller list in Germany and here in America they are prescribed reading in the German course in practically all colleges. Some of his chapters, such as his "Opera Guide," have become classics: He attempts to tell the stories of the more difficult and implausible operas—all seen from the point of view of the tenor.

"Lohengrin arrives in his silver armour and every spotlight is turned on him. Looking like an electrical reflector, he sings the swan song, a little off pitch. The swan hears it and leaves." He describes the beginning of the third act: "When the curtain rises on the bridal chamber, the audience knows right away that this will be a very uncomfortable wedding night, because the only piece of furniture is a bench in the window."

And now, on the plane, winging back home, I began to read his letters. They are remarkable documents. It's the whole war, as seen from the other side, through the eyes of a man who detested the fascist system, who hated the Nazis with a white fury. In the midst of the astonishing German victories in the early part of the war he was firmly convinced that Hitler MUST and WOULD lose. He dreaded communism, and all his predictions have come true. He told of all the spying that went on, the denunciations to the Gestapo, the sudden disappearances of innocent people, of the daily new edicts and restrictions, of confiscations that were nothing but robberies, arrests, and executions; how every crime committed was draped in the mantilla of legality.

His great perception, intelligence, decency, his wonderful humanity, his love of music and above all his worshipful adoration for his Elsa—through every page they shimmered with luminescent radiance.

It was dawn when I finished reading his letters. On the horizon the coast of Brazil became visible. I sat very quietly, with a feeling of serene happiness and gratitude that fate had chosen these two particular people as my parents. And my heart went back to the small plot of earth, nestling against the village church in Egern on the Tegernsee, where they slept. On their grave are inscribed the last two lines of a song "Es muss ein Wunderbares sein . . ." by Franz Liszt, which Papa always sang for my mother:

Vom ersten Kuss bis in den Tod
Sich nur von Liebe sagen.

From first embrace until the last
Love was their only language.

Larchmont April 8, 1962